# NEWPOR

*A Short History*

A Topographical CHART of the
BAY of NARRAGANSET in the Province of NEW ENGLAND,
with all the ISLES contained therein, among which
RHODE ISLAND and CONNONICUT
have been particularly SURVEYED.
Shewing the true position & bearings of the Banks, Shoals, Rocks &c. as likewise the Soundings
To which have been added the several Works & Batteries raised by the Americans.
Taken by Order of the PRINCIPAL FARMERS on Rhode Island.
By CHARLES BLASKOWITZ.
Engraved & Printed for Wm. FADEN, Charing Cross, as the Act directs July 22d 1777.
SCALE of Statute Miles

# NEWPORT

## A Short History

C.P.B. Jefferys

Revised by the Publications Committee
of the Newport Historical Society

NEWPORT HISTORICAL SOCIETY

Front cover, clockwise from upper left: Doorway on Spring Street, photo from Stock Newport, by Onne Van Der Wal; The J-boats *Endeavour* and *Shamrock V*, © Daniel Forster; Aerial View of "The Breakers," courtesy of the Preservation Society of Newport County, photo by Richard Cheek; The Newport Casino Interior Court and Tower, courtesy of the International Tennis Hall of Fame at the Newport Casino, Newport, Rhode Island.

Back cover, clockwise from upper left: Edith Wharton, Sir Thomas Lipton, Abraham Redwood, The Rev. Reed Family, Mrs. Austin Sands, Rear Admiral Stephen B. Luce, Julia Sands, William Trost Richards, Judah Touro, John Howard Benson. From the collection of the Newport Historical Society.

Frontispiece, "A Topographical Chart of the Bay of Narragansett in the Province of New England, with all the Isles contained therein, amoung which Rhode Island and Connonicut have been particularly Surveyed . . ." by Charles Blaskowitz, ca.1777.

Originally published in 1976 as *NEWPORT 1639-1976, An Historical Sketch* by C.P.B. Jefferys under the auspices of the Newport Historical Society. Revised by the Publications Committee of the Newport Historical Society 1992.

Designer: Jane Carey, Newport, RI
Printer: Hamilton Printing Company, Portsmouth, RI

Library of Congress Cataloging-in-Publication Data
Jefferys, C.P.B. (Charles Peter Beauchamp), 1898-1980
    Newport: a short history / C.P.B. Jefferys;
    revised by the Publications Committee of the
    Newport Historical Society.
    p. 116 cm.
    Rev. ed. of: Newport 1639-1976. 1976.
    Includes index.
    ISBN 0-9633200-0-9 pbk.
    ISBN 0-9633200-1-7 special binding
    1. Newport (RI)—History. I. Jefferys, C.P.B. (Charles Peter Beauchamp), 1898-1980.
    Newport 1639-1976. II. Newport Historical Society. Publications Committee. III. Title.
    F89.N5J44 1992
    974.5'6—dc20                    92-19741 CIP

# Contents

# Preface to the Present Edition

In 1976 C.P.B. Jefferys, the President of the Newport Historical Society, who taught history at nearby St. George's School, wrote an introduction for Florence Simister's book *Streets of the City*, in which he divided Newport's three and a half centuries into six periods. Both the book for which it was written and the introduction itself proved to be so popular that Jefferys was persuaded by friends and associates at the Newport Historical Society to expand his thoughts into a "vest pocket" short history of Newport. He framed the resulting *Newport, 1639-1976; An Historical Sketch* with an eye to entertaining as well as informing.

In 1989, as Newport celebrated the 350th anniversary of its founding, the Newport Historical Society, realizing the popularity of "Cham" Jefferys' book, decided to revise and republish it. The task of this revision was given to the Publications Committee, which oversees the publication of the Historical Society's quarterly journal *Newport History*. Members of the Committee were: Dr. Howard S. Browne, Chairman, Mrs. Peter Bolhouse, Dr. John B. Hattendorf, Mrs. John H. Howard, Dr. William Robinson, Rear Admiral John R. Wadleigh, Eileen Warburton, along with the Historical Society's president, Samuel M.C. Barker, and Nancy Ellen Giorgi, staff editor. In addition to assisting the Committee on a number of matters, Nancy generated the index for the book. M. Joan Youngken, the Society's Collections Manager, provided most of the illustrations. Bertram Lippincott III, the Society's Librarian, helped verify the accuracy of our information. The responsibilities of general editor of the project were assigned to the Society's Executive Director, Daniel Snydacker, Jr. Along with a comprehensive revision of Jefferys' text, the Publications Committee also wrote a short introduction which more fully sets the stage for the founding of Newport in 1639.

As Jefferys made clear in his own preface to the book, it was not a "scholarly treatise," and this revision is aimed at continuing the general tone Jefferys himself took. Nevertheless, it was necessary to correct the errors in Jefferys' original and expand on some areas which Jefferys treated only in passing. Jefferys was very close in time to the events he wrote about in his final chapter, and additional work had to be done to bring this chapter up to the level of the remainder of the work.

History never stops — and much has happened in Newport between 1976 and 1991. Rear Admiral John R. Wadleigh, USN, retired, a member of the Publications Committee, wrote a new concluding chapter to bring the book up to date. Admiral Wadleigh has been a frequent contributor to *Newport History* and was co-author, along with John B. Hattendorf and B. Mitchell Simpson III, of *Sailors and Scholars: The Centennial History of the U.S. Naval War College* (Newport, 1984). Hattendorf, who is Ernest J. King Professor of Maritime History at the Naval War College, is also a member of the Society's Publications Committee and was of great assistance in the revision of Jefferys' book.

The book's title was changed, illustrations were chosen and the book itself redesigned. Through all these changes, however, the Publications Committee strove to keep the book both affordable and of interest to the reader who wants an introduction to the history of one of America's most historic cities.

Funding for the book was provided by the generous support of a number of friends of the Newport Historical Society — some old and some new. The late Alan T. Schumacher, a long time friend, left the Society a generous bequest in his will which was applied to the publishing cost. Alan had written a review of C.P.B. Jefferys' original book in 1976 for *Newport History*, the Society's journal, in which he wrote "It can confidently be said, as the book answers a definite need, that copies will not only be sold in the bicentennial year but for a long time to come in various editions." These words have proven prophetic, and how appropriate that Alan was able to make a posthumous contribution to the current edition.

New friends as well have helped us with the current revision. Elizabeth Meyer made a significant contribution toward the cost of publication. The Bank of Newport was gracious enough to provide a no-interest loan which enabled us to meet the start-up costs of the project. Without the support of these generous benefactors, and the support of the membership of the Newport Historical Society, this volume would not have been possible.

*For Gladys Bolhouse*
*who, more than anyone,*
*has helped keep Newport's history alive.*

*Ninigret, a sachem of the Narragansett Indians, by an anonymous 17th-century artist ca. 1681.* Museum of Art, Rhode Island School of Design, gift of Mr. Robert Winthrop.

# Introduction

## NATIVE AMERICANS AND
## THE EUROPEAN VOYAGES OF DISCOVERY

Newport is the southernmost of three towns on Aquidneck Island with Portsmouth, the first to be settled, at the northern part. The meaning of the Indian name "Aquidneck" is obscure but said to mean "at the Island" or, according to an author of the Victorian era, "Isle of Peace." The 16th-century Italian explorer Giovanni da Verrazzano spoke of Block Island as being about the size of the Island of Rhodes in the Mediterranean. Verrazzano sailed for the King of France between 1524 and 1528 on the first recorded and documented voyage to explore the coast of North America from Florida to Newfoundland, and he anchored in Newport Harbor for fifteen days.

Roger Williams, the founder of the colony of Rhode Island, read a translation of Verrazzano's account in Richard Hakluyt's *Principal Navigations* and mistakenly thought Verrazzano was referring to Aquidneck Island rather than Block Island. In 1637 Williams named the Island, and in 1644 a Court of Election for Newport and Portsmouth confirmed Williams' choice by adopting "Ile of Rhods or Rhod-Island" as the official name. A century later, in 1743, the third town on the Island, Middletown, seceded from Newport and received a town

*Giovanni da Verrazzano, whose account of his exploration of Narragansett Bay in 1524 was read by Roger Williams before he founded Providence. Bridges named after this explorer are found in both New York and Rhode Island.* The Pierpont Morgan Library, New York. (MA776).

XI

*The Old Stone Mill in an early undated photograph.* NHS collection.

charter of its own. In 1663 King Charles II's charter joined Rhode Island with Providence and the official name of the colony, now the state, is Rhode Island and Providence Plantations, the longest name for the smallest state. Until the present century the courthouses at Newport, Providence, Kingstown, East Greenwich and Bristol were all officially alternate meeting places for the General Assembly.

The first settlers on the Island were, of course, not European, but rather the Wampanoags, a tribe of the Algonquian language group. These people practiced a diversified blend of agriculture, hunting and fishing. At the time of the first European contact with the area, however, the Wampanoags were being forced northward off the Island by the Narragansetts, who had a more highly developed political structure and superior seafaring skills. The Narragansetts' sphere of influence extended from just east of the Connecticut River to the Sakonnet River and included Block Island, where they raised bumper crops of corn.

A number of explorers sailed into or past Narragansett Bay long before the first English settlers. Wishful thinkers like to regard the Vikings as the earliest, and point to the Old Stone Mill in Touro Park as evidence. This so-called "Viking Tower" is more likely the remains of a 17th-century stone mill which stands on property formerly owned by Governor Benedict Arnold. Most historians agree that it was the base of the Governor's mill and not a Viking stone tower, or a Portuguese or Irish chapel. In addition to Verrazzano, early explorers also include the Dutchman Adrien Bloeck, for whom Block Island was ultimately named, as well as minor English traders such as John Oldham, who was murdered by the Pequot Indians in 1635. Some scholars claim that the Portuguese explorer Miguel Corte Real left his mark in 1511 on Dighton Rock up the Taunton River.

*Model of the Great Friends Meeting House in Newport as it looked when first constructed in 1699. This building, currently owned by the Newport Historical Society, was the location of the New England Yearly Meeting until the early 20th century.* Photograph by John Corbett.

# CHAPTER

# 1

# Newport Begins
# 1639-1700

The first European settlers on Aquidneck Island were led by the famous "Antinomian" Anne Hutchinson who had, like Roger Williams before her, been banished from the Massachusetts Bay Colony for her radical religious views. She brought with her a loyal group of followers, including her husband, and they purchased land from the Narragansett sachems Canonicus and Miantonomi in 1638 for ten coats and twenty hoes. The native inhabitants were "required to remove themselves from off the Island before the next winter."

This small group settled first on the northern tip of Aquidneck near the area known as Common Fence Point. They took the Narragansett name of Pocasset for their settlement, but almost from the beginning religious disagreements began to divide this first settlement and by the next year a group led by Nicholas Easton and William Coddington, along with Dr. John Clarke, moved from the northern to the southern tip of the Island, where they founded Newport in 1639.

## RELIGIOUS TOLERATION

The "Newport Compact," dated April 1639, which formed the basis of the settlement, was signed by John Clarke (pastor, physician and statesman), William Coddington (merchant and legislator), William Dyer (clerk and later attorney general), Nicholas Easton (farmer, miller, tanner and builder), John Coggeshall and William Brenton (elders and farmer-merchants), Henry Bull (peace officer), Jeremy Clarke (surveyor-merchant) and Thomas Hazard. Five of these were eventually chosen as presidents or governors of Aquidneck and the colony.

1

This early document established the basis for the religious toleration for which Newport quickly became well known. Dr. John Clarke, who went as a young man from England to the Massachusetts Bay Colony, should be given credit for this liberal religious policy. His political and religious views and his association with Anne Hutchinson were instrumental in convincing the small band of settlers to commit their settlement to the "lively experiment" in religious liberty begun by Roger Williams.

The colony's explicit commitment to religious tolerance soon brought a stream of religious groups seeking sanctuary from the banishments and persecution they suffered elsewhere in colonies as well as in Europe. This religious diversity became a hallmark of Newport society through the rest of the colonial period. Foremost among these early groups attracted to Newport in the 17th century by its religious toleration were the Jews and Quakers who had been banished and persecuted elsewhere in the Atlantic world. Both groups flourished in Newport's tolerant atmosphere and went on to dominate the town's economy and society in the following century.

Historians disagree on the exact date, but in approximately 1658 Moses Pacheco, Mordecai Campanall and other Jews from Curaçao, recognizing the unique opportunities presented to them by these remarkably tolerant attitudes, began to settle in the village and purchased a burial ground. The Jews were granted the freedom to practice their religion, but they were systematically denied the vote until the end of the 18th century.

The Society of Friends, called Quakers by their detractors, after being expelled from New Amsterdam (1657), were also allowed to settle in this haven. The Plymouth Colony's appeal to Rhode Island to bar them was rejected. In 1672 the great Quaker missionary George Fox came to Newport to attend the yearly meeting. On August 6, 1672, Roger Williams who, by that point, had become a Baptist, rowed his own skiff all the way from Providence, taking all night and part of the day, to carry on a well-publicized debate with Fox, William Edmundson and other Quakers. Unfortunately, and perhaps to avoid confrontation with Williams, Fox left the Island before Williams arrived.

In 1660 a group of Seventh Day Baptists organized in Newport. Their second meetinghouse, built in 1729, is preserved as part of the Newport Historical Society's headquarters. Among the last of the major denominations to arrive, Anglicans petitioned the British authorities to establish a church here in 1698. Encouraged by the Society for the Propagation of the Gospel in Foreign Parts, their first meetinghouse was replaced by the current Trinity Church, which was built in 1725-26. The Congregationalists, Paedobaptists and other Protestant groups are said to have dwelt together in reasonable harmony. The Presbyterian Samuel Maverick described the village as "a receptacle for people of several sorts of opinions . . .," while some of the Boston divines were far less moderate in their comments: the "receptacle" becomes a "sewer."

## EARLY AGRICULTURE

Like New Amsterdam and Boston, the village of Newport was settled on a good, well-protected harbor. Unlike these two cities, which were at the same time both Newport's partners and rivals in commerce, the Island, from the beginning, had a thriving agricultural society. A surplus of sheep, cattle, hogs, horses, foodstuffs and salt fish led to a prosperous seventeenth-century merchant-farmer social structure. The soil of the farms of the Island was fertile, and the wealthy settlers such as Brenton, Coggeshall, Coddington, Easton and others who received large grants of land adapted the farming techniques of Old England to the Island's needs. They were taught by the Narragansetts that corn was an excellent food, but discovered that it was also good feed for their livestock. Grain was grown in sufficient quantity for home consumption as well as to feed cattle and horses for export. Common grazing land was cleared and sheep thrived on the Island to such an extent that the official seal of the Council of Newport was wrought with a sheep in the center and inscribed "seal of the Newport Rhode Island Council." This seventeenth-century seal is one of the earliest works of a silversmith in the New England colonies and is now in the collection of the Newport Historical Society.

The little village of Newport prospered so well that it soon grew into one of the five largest cities in British America along with Boston, Philadelphia, Charles Town, South Carolina (so spelled until

*Seal of the Town of Newport made in 1696 by Arnold Collins (?-1735), one of Rhode Island's first silversmiths.* NHS65.3.1.

around 1783) and the Dutch New Amsterdam. The half-century after its founding saw the settlers clearing and settling the land, creating a political organization and establishing the principle of separate church and state with official tolerance for almost all religious beliefs. The settlers were able, through their good relations with the Indians, to avoid any fighting on Aquidneck Island during the destructive King Philip's War (1675-1676). The founders were shrewd beyond their time in realizing the superiority of persuasion over compulsion.


## THE LANDSCAPE OF 17TH-CENTURY NEWPORT

Aquidneck is approximately fifteen miles from north to south. Shaped like a boot, the Island varies in width from one to three miles. Sandy beaches with changing shallows have been formed by the steady surf rolling in from the Atlantic. The chemical properties of a red seaweed, which accumulates at certain times of the year, have been used through three centuries to fertilize and enrich the good earth. The many small coves on Narragansett Bay and the Sakonnet Passage have given refuge to generations of fishermen and inter-island traders as well as smugglers and in more recent times, bootleggers, as well as to yachtsmen and small boat sailors.

The common English origin of the early settlers tended to unite them with Boston, Philadelphia and later with Charleston, but not with the Dutch in New Amsterdam. The latter became a bitter commercial rival to Newport, each struggling to gain ascendancy. The first European settlers moved into a landscape that had already been altered significantly by the Wampanoags and the Narragansetts. Fields had been cleared for growing corn and other crops and the underbrush in woodlands was burned to create a habitat favorable for the deer and other game they hunted for meat. Cleared pathways linked the sites of their various encampments with fields and the beaches where they went to fish. Many of these footpaths were taken over as Newport's first roads and streets.

The two original streets, Thames and Marlborough, were laid out in 1654. Luckily these two have been allowed to keep their original names, although part of Thames Street has been vastly changed in recent years. America's Cup Avenue now winds its way behind the original waterfront.

*The Wanton-Lyman-Hazard House was built ca. 1675 for Stephen Mumford, a Seventh Day Baptist minister. Its sharply pitched roof, central chimney and asymmetrical facade identify it as a vernacular Rhode Island floorplan structure. It is the oldest surviving house in Newport and is owned by the Newport Historical Society.* Photograph by John T. Hopf.

Soon the crude huts of the first period were replaced by substantial homes of wood. Timber was plentiful. By 1680 Newport had about 400 houses, approximately two-thirds of them located within the village itself. The one-room, end-chimney pioneer house was replaced by the central-chimney type with at least two rooms on each floor — one noticeably larger than the other. The Wanton-Lyman-Hazard House, owned by the Newport Historical Society and built about 1675, is an excellent example of this layout which would later become known as the Rhode Island floor plan. At least four other buildings in Newport date before 1700; the Old Stone Mill, the White Horse Tavern, the Friends Meeting House and the Mawdsley House at the corner of Spring and John Street.

## THE KING CHARLES II CHARTER OF 1663

Rhode Island and Connecticut were unique in that they were the only two North American British colonies without a Royal Governor. Although many of the political institutions in local government were taken from the mother country, the colony was unique in that it was a virtual democracy, where "freemen" (or those who met the land qualification for voting privileges) were allowed to vote directly for the laws and ordinances which governed them. With its Town Meeting system, Newport enjoyed considerable local autonomy. The selectmen or town council were relatively successful in the attempt to secure needed powers, more so than in most other colonies.

In 1644 Parliament granted a charter to Newport, Portsmouth and Providence thanks to the efforts of William Coddington. Unfortunately for the rest of the settlers, Coddington had himself named "President of the Colony for life," and immediately a delegation was dispatched back to England to have this revoked. In 1663, after the Restoration, King Charles II granted a new and very liberal charter which deposed Coddington and guaranteed self government. This charter remained the constitution of the Colony and later the State of Rhode Island and Providence Plantations for 179 years until its revision in 1843.

The village of Newport was built on an extremely successful foundation. After only four decades there were distinct signs of an emerging prosperous urban society. During this pioneer period the community grew from approximately 100 persons in 1640 to 2500 in 1680. Newport had few if any paupers before King Philip's War, but the refugees who came from Providence, Wickford, Warwick and elsewhere to escape danger numbered several hundred. These became a severe burden on the Quakers whose policy throughout the war had been to make the Island a safe refuge. Many poor remained after the danger was over and a regular "poor rate" was levied to help take care of them. Wood was the only fuel used for heating and even the poor, using pine knots and "light wood," were able to keep reasonably warm.

Immediately upon the settlement of Newport, the founders made provisions for a school and hired Robert Lenthal to be its master. Urged by Coddington, Coggeshall and Brenton, formerly large contributors to the Boston school fund, the Town Meeting in 1640 set aside 100 acres for the "encouragement of the poorer sort to train up their youth in learning." This is the earliest land grant that any of the English colonies had set aside as a permanent endowment for education. A qualified schoolmaster was soon called to keep the public school. One of his successors was Robert, brother of Roger Williams, and in 1683 a schoolhouse was built. The Quakers also allowed their meeting house to be used as a private school until 1686.

*Captain Thomas Dring, painted by Ludwig Hirschmann, 1793. Dring was a merchant and a sea captain as is clearly evident from the telescope he is holding and the ship in the background over his shoulder. Both were icons of his occupation that were commonly used in portraits of those involved with maritime trade.* NHS67.3.

# 2

# The Thriving Colonial Seaport
# 1700-1770

Thanks to an ideal climate and a magnificent, accessible harbor, the young village grew into affluent maturity. Newport eventually became the metropolis of the Colony of Rhode Island and Providence Plantations. In town meeting, the growing town became the first in British North America to adopt a plan to name its streets. To aid outsiders and encourage commerce, the Town Meeting chose John Mumford, surveyor, to make a map on which the streets were named.

The Great Meeting House of the Society of Friends (1699) was the most substantial building in town. Restored between 1961 and 1974, it is now owned by the Newport Historical Society. New England Quakers built and later enlarged it to accommodate their Yearly Meeting. The Newport Friends in the early 18th century were a numerous and strong element in a population of approximately 3000. In naming the streets in the Point section, which they owned, they were influenced by William Penn, the Pennsylvania Quaker, who, wishing to avoid "man worship" by naming streets after individuals, renamed the streets of Philadelphia. They used the names of trees, such as walnut and poplar, in naming the streets running east and west and numbers to designate those running north and south.

At the turn of the century more lands were set aside by the Town Meeting to support the town school, and the new schoolmaster was required to teach three or four orphans free before he could benefit from the land grant endowment. A new school was built at town expense, and Newport with its Latin School and a teacher of the "arts of writing and arithmetic" supported all branches of secondary education then in vogue. The land Dr. John Clarke left in his will for "schooling children of the poor" now lies within Middletown and was known as Charity Farm before being divided into an industrial park. Income from this legacy, the earliest of its kind in America, legally must be used to support public education. This remarkable will is in the archives of the Newport Historical Society. The Newport Friends in 1711 built their own school in order to avoid "ye corrupt ways, manners, fashions and Tongue of ye world." There were other private schools in Newport, but the excellent boarding schools of Boston made them less in demand.

## NEWPORT'S 18TH-CENTURY ECONOMY

In the seaport town itself, making a living occupied the inhabitants of all classes. Shipping steadily increased in importance and created various related jobs. Many men went to sea as mariners in the crew of Newport based ships. Mechanics and artisans were kept busy pursuing their trades, and shopkeepers were busy supplying their neighbors' necessities. New mills, breweries, distilleries, bakeries, cooperages and tanneries appeared and multiplied as trade increased, and the volume of shipbuilding compared favorably with that of Boston. Newport started with small and inexpensive boats which could be delivered quickly but soon was building ocean-going vessels. In 1712 there were more than a dozen shipyards in Newport. Timber was plentiful and carpenters, joiners, shipwrights and other artisans united in building these tall ships. Ropewalks, which are clearly visible on the maps of the period, and sail lofts employed other skilled artisans. The townsfolk who had employment in Newport were, of course, ultimately dependent for their daily bread on farms surrounding the town. As Newport's exports increased there was more and more demand for the products of millers, bakers, butchers, packers and coopers.

## THE GROWING POPULATION

During this period the population in Newport grew rapidly. A conservative estimate shows that in 1710 Newport had a population of 2800; ten years later, 3800; in 1730, 4600 and twelve years later in 1742, 6200, or a 65% increase in 32 years. The racial and national composition of the population also underwent some changes. In 1730 African-Americans made up almost 14% of the population and Indians only 3%. By 1755, the Black population had risen to 18% of the total. The 1774 tax census shows that roughly one-third of the middle class in

Newport owned at least one slave and many families owned five or more. These slaves lived in the households of their owners and many of them worked for wages outside of the household in addition to helping with the labor-intensive work of running a colonial home.

By the mid-18th century, the religious diversity that grew out of the colony's toleration was evident to contemporaries and an important part of what made the town unique. Religion and family combined to become the most powerful influence on life in Newport. The two in combination often determined with whom one did business, marriage prospects and even the political stance taken by individuals on the eve of the Revolution. By then there were three different Baptist churches, Episcopalians, Congregationalists, Quakers, Jews and Moravians all thriving in Newport. A few French Huguenots emigrated to Newport and found a home. By mid century, however, the population mix had stabilized and the Governor of Rhode Island reported back to England that "We have lately a few or no new comers either of English, Scotch, Irish, or foreigners."

Crime was not a serious problem during these transitional years. The prison was shamefully neglected and escapes were more the rule than the exception. The Town Council spent only twenty shillings "towards ye repair of ye prison" and soon it was in such dilapidated condition that prisoners could escape practically at will. Several inmates fled in the 1730s and left an insulting message for the prison keeper chalked on the floor. A more effective deterrence for crime seems to have been the appointment of a "town whipper" to preside over the whipping post and later the stocks in the "Upper Market." Sexual promiscuity was not uncommon and prostitution was accepted as a part of urban society. In this, the seaport town of Newport was no exception. However, according to an 18th-century traveler, Newport gentlemen met their paramours more discreetly than was the case on the streets of Boston, Manhattan, or Philadelphia.

The rapid growth of the town meant that taverns, victual houses and grog shops multiplied to meet demand. Approximately twenty taverns were licensed annually. The Nichols' White Horse Tavern was — and still is — a popular gathering place. The Friends would drop in after Meeting, the Town Council held its meetings there (1713-1714), and it was a convenient hostel for the out-of-town members of the Assembly. This was true in spite of the fact that one visitor from the South in 1744 complained of "bugs." This tavern has been restored and, after a brief period of management by the Preservation Society of Newport County, is now privately owned and again a popular tavern with a colonial atmosphere. Other excellent public houses served sumptuous meals: Palmer, Mallet and Melville were notable hosts. Whiting's "King's Arms" was noted as a meeting place where prominent merchants and shipbuilders could transact business. Sarah Bright provided a billiard table, a nine-pin alley and a large garden for her patrons.

As this transitional period came to an end, Newport streets were badly neglected and resembled barnyards. Swine had been forbidden to roam on the thoroughfares, but dogs, dead or alive, were a menace in spite of two town dogcatchers. An ordinance was passed to limit ownership of dogs to owners of real estate, but dogs continued to be a serious problem. Traffic was another problem; "fast and hard riding of horses" in the streets of the town led to many injuries to children. In spite of an earlier ordinance levying a fine for reckless driving, stronger laws had to be passed to compensate for death caused by cart or horse. Children were in great danger of being run over by cart wheels.

When Newport was hardly more than a rambling village it lost only an occasional house to fire. A close call was a threatening blaze in 1705 which broke out in a smithy but was confined to one nearby house. A few years later a group of prominent men formed a fire club and purchased leather buckets and a fire engine. The town took over the care of this equipment but the members of the club complained of careless neglect by the town. The greatest scare came in February 1730 when a fire on Malbone's wharf destroyed a cooper's shop and six warehouses. An eyewitness tells us that there was no loss of life and a general fire was prevented "through God's wonderful mercy."

Soon after this Newport's wealthiest citizen, Godfrey Malbone, donated a new suction type engine, "Torrent No. 1," made in London. Engine Companies had orders to inspect and "try" their machines regularly and at any outcry of "Fire" to "bring out ye engines." An ordinance was passed in Town Meeting requiring every citizen to possess a leather bucket with his name painted on it. A strong support for efficient fire prevention was the Heart-in-Hand Fire Company, a club with a socially exclusive membership. It was modeled after a similar one in Boston. Other clubs had such names as "Hand-in-Hand," "United," "Rough and Ready," "Hercules," "Hope," "Protection," and "Deluge." As in more recent times, Newport had volunteer firemen whose equipment was partly owned by individual citizens and clubs and partly by the town. The combination proved amazingly efficient.

It was not until 1885 that the city organized a full-time Fire Department, which has grown with the city from the exciting horse-drawn steam pumpers belching smoke to modern and efficient trucks, pumpers, huge hook-and-ladders and rescue wagons with such expertly trained rescue teams that it has been called one of the best in New England.

## TRANSPORTATION AND TRADE

From the earliest days the Island's economic and social life was dependent upon transportation. Freight vessels of all kinds carried its products abroad. Smaller sail ferries connected the Island with Saunderstown, Jamestown, Bristol and Tiverton.

Like so many other features of 17th- and 18th-century Newport's history, the town's development as a trading port followed religious pathways. In the 1650s, groups of both Quakers and Jews came to Newport in search of religious toleration. Most of the Jews were Sephardic. They had been expelled from Spain or Portugal in 1492 when Christians forced the Islamic leaders out as well. These Jews, who had been in exile ever since, came to Newport by way of Barbados, Jamaica, Surinam, Curaçao, and Amsterdam. The Quakers came from Barbados, New York, and England. Both groups left behind them a trail of communities of co-religionists with whom they continued to be in contact for religious and commercial affairs. These trails became the basis of Newport's trade routes during the colonial period, and the Quakers and Jews dominated the town's maritime trade until the 1760s. At that time Newport's wealthiest men were Aaron Lopez, a Jew, and Abraham Redwood, a Quaker.

During the 17th and 18th centuries, society in Rhode Island was more like that of the Chesapeake region than that of the rest of New England, allowing its inhabitants a certain license to pursue individual gain through commerce and trade more aggressively than their fellow New Englanders. This helped propel Newport by the mid-18th century into its position as one of the top five ports in colonial America along with Boston, New York, Philadelphia, and Charlestown, South Carolina.

During this century, between 1660 and 1760, despite Newport's reputation for lawlessness and the slave trade, the reality was that the vast majority of the town's trade consisted of rather pedestrian but nevertheless lucrative shuttle voyages back and forth between Newport and the West Indies on the one hand, and coastal voyages to Boston, New York, Philadelphia and Charlestown, South Carolina, on the other. Merchants brought English goods, molasses, lumber and other raw materials into Newport and shipped out finished products like rum, spermaceti candles and furniture. In only three years,

*Trade sign for Isaac Stelle's whale oil chandlery. The sign shows the essential elements of Stelle's business: large wooden barrels known as hogsheads (52.5 gallons) in which the oil was shipped, schooners, and a workhouse where the oil was melted down and purified. On the reverse of the sign is a breaching whale being pursued by a whaleboat.* From the collection of Mystic Seaport Museum 38.15.

between 1764 and 1767, 492 chairs, 71 case pieces and 30 tables entered Annapolis, Maryland, and 133 chairs, 70 case pieces and 30 tables entered Charleston, South Carolina, all from Newport.

As Newport's affluent merchants expanded their commercial ventures, shipbuilding, privateering, whaling and, on the seamy side, smuggling and the now notorious triangular trade of molasses, rum and slaves brought profits that led to a new wealthy class of entrepreneurs and merchant princes. Because of the almost continuous wars with France beginning in 1689, privateering was especially profitable. Thomas Tew used Newport as a "free port for pirates" and brought in one cargo said to be worth £100,000. In this "golden age" Newport merchants caused their Boston rivals to complain of recession and high taxes while they wrested a large share of the Caribbean commerce from them. They made rum from West Indian molasses, and while most of this potent commodity was shipped to other coastal cities and towns, some of it made its way into the slave trade. Boston, however, still held the advantage in direct trade with Europe. Communication over land between these two emerging cities of New England was vastly improved with better roads. Scheduled private carriers made round trips with "Goods, Merchandize, Books, Men, Women, and Children."

Newport shipbuilding was extremely profitable and, under the leadership of men of the merchant class, many of them Quakers, the city hummed with shipyards and ropewalks. Almost all the 600 sailing ships owned by the merchants of Newport had been constructed locally. Some of the merchants were specialists: Stephen Ayrault in hardware and Peter Bours in slave traffic. Many lived like princes on their own estates on Aquidneck Island or in other parts of the colony.

## THE CULTURAL LIFE OF 18TH-CENTURY NEWPORT

The seeds of culture thrive in wealth, and this was certainly true in 18th-century Newport. George Berkeley, philosopher and Dean of Derry, was sent by the Society for the Propagation of the Gospel in Foreign Parts to start a college in Bermuda, partially for the education of the Indians. While waiting in vain for Parliament to fund the project, Berkeley came to Newport. In 1729 he purchased land and built his home, "Whitehall," in what is now Middletown. Hanging Rock, overlooking Second Beach not far from the house, is said to be the site where Berkeley wrote one of his better-known works, *Alciphron*.

Berkeley also brought with him a small coterie of intellectuals and artists which included John Smibert the painter. These recent arrivals found an active group of cultural leaders in Newport including Abraham Redwood, Henry Collins and others who by their charm and intellectual prowess helped to mold this city by the sea into a center of culture.

Berkeley returned home in 1731 and was later consecrated Bishop of Cloyne. He left "Whitehall" to Yale University when he departed. During his short stay in America he was active in forming a literary and philosophical society. Some of this group became founders and charter members of the Redwood Library and Athenaeum in 1746-1747. Abraham Redwood, a wealthy merchant who came to Newport from Antigua, gave £500 to be used to purchase "useful books suitable for a Public Library. . . having nothing in view but the Good of Mankind." Redwood persuaded his fellow incorporators to build the library on land donated by another wealthy merchant, Henry Collins.

Peter Harrison was chosen to design the building. Born in York, England, Harrison emigrated to Newport in 1740 at the age of twenty-three. He took the church-temple design of the library from an illustration of a domed garden pavilion in *Andrea Palladio's Architecture in Four Books*, by Edward Hoppus and Benjamin Cole. The library's original collection was purchased in London but was dispersed during the Revolution. It was retrieved by the library after the war and is now largely intact. Redwood became the third library of its kind in North America. The first was the Library Company of Philadelphia, founded by Benjamin Franklin in 1731. The Redwood opened in 1750 and remains the oldest subscription library to survive in its original building.

This community, with a good library to foster literary and philosophical discussions, also supported an enlightened press. James Franklin, older brother of Benjamin, was the first printer in Newport. Before coming to Newport, he published the *New England Courant*, a Boston paper noted for supporting unpopular causes. Soon after the *Courant* was forced to close, James moved to Newport. The Franklin Press, founded in 1729, was one of the earliest in America. After James's death in 1735 his widow Ann continued publication, bringing up her daughters and son James as printers. In 1758 the first issue of the *Newport Mercury* was printed on Franklin's press. It was, and still is, a weekly newspaper and enjoys an international circulation. The Widow Franklin and Samuel Hall, whom she later took in as a partner, were also responsible for most of the almanacs of the day. The *Mercury* was sold to Solomon Southwick in 1768. The motto of the

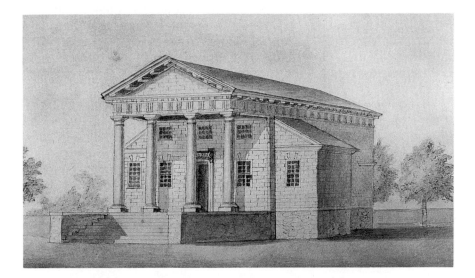

*Redwood Library and Athenaeum, designed by Newport architect Peter Harrison in 1748. This engraving was made from a drawing by Pierre Eugene du Simitiere, who visited Newport in 1768.* Courtesy of the Philadelphia Library Company.

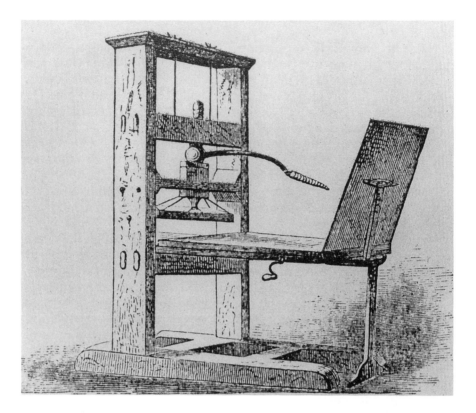

*Engraving of James Franklin's press from* Harper's New Monthly Magazine, *August 1854. This press was used for printing the* Newport Mercury, *Newport's first newspaper, as well as books, broadsides and even currency for the colonial government.*

journal became "Undaunted by TYRANTS we'll DIE or be FREE." A varied collection of literary works and broadsides carry the imprint of these early Newport printers.

No account of Newport's intellectual life during the 18th century would be complete without Ezra Stiles, the minister who was called to the Second Congregational Church in 1756 and went on, after he fled Newport on the eve of the British occupation of the town during the Revolution, to become one of Yale University's most distinguished early presidents. Stiles was also elected Librarian of Redwood Library, and the diaries he kept while in Newport reveal a truly brilliant, cosmopolitan intellect as well as many fascinating details about life in Newport at the time.

## ILLNESS AND COLONIAL MEDICINE

Despite Newport's reputation for a healthy climate, smallpox epidemics took many lives in the colonial period. Dr. Thomas Rodman treated the smallpox cases in an isolation hospital on Coaster's Harbor Island, site of the present Naval War College. Trinity Church paid Dr. Thomas Eyres to look after Newport's Black families. Inoculation for smallpox was voted down in Town Meeting for fear that it would spread the disease. Influential citizens such as Ezra Stiles, Dr. Cyrus Johnson, Martin Howard, Thomas Vernon, Silas Cook, Dr. Rodman and Gideon Cornell petitioned for it without success. Newporters went off the Island for immunization, and it was not until 1782 that Newport allowed inoculations. Drs. Jonathan Easton, Benjamin Mason and Isaac Senter divided the work.

Inoculation provided immunity from smallpox, although the death rate from the mild form of the disease that resulted was as high as five percent. Dr. Benjamin Waterhouse, one of the founders and professor of medicine at Harvard Medical School, was another Newporter who made medical history in the fight against smallpox. Born in Newport in 1754, he was educated in Newport's school system and received his first medical training from Dr. John Halliburton, also of Newport. Waterhouse was the first to vaccinate in the Western Hemisphere. Vaccination, discovered by Edward Jenner in England, provided a much more effective and safer immunity to this dread scourge than inoculation.

Thomas Moffat and William Hunter were two other noted medical men in Newport during this period. Both came from Scotland. Moffat once found himself in court paying child support as the father of a child by one Mary Wheatley. To supplement his income during his early years in practice, Moffat bought a snuff mill in Narragansett and employed the father of artist Gilbert Stuart to manage it, and Moffat encouraged the young Stuart in his painting. Moffat's home was furnished with fine paintings, china, furniture, silver and other valuables. He was the second librarian of the Redwood Library and Athenaeum, and, as was the case with many of those involved with Redwood, Moffat was a staunch Tory. He served as one of the commissioners of the Stamp Act and, during the Stamp Act riots in 1765, the mob sacked Moffat's Newport house and forced him to flee. He took refuge in the house of the Quaker Thomas Robinson on Washington Street and once the riots were over made his way to New London. From there he fled to London where he later died.

William Hunter, another Loyalist, came from Scotland in 1752. He was an excellent and innovative physician. In 1754 he gave the first lectures in the colonies on surgery and anatomy at the Colony House.

*Robert Feke (1705-1750). Feke was one of the best-known early portrait artists in Newport.* NHS P600.

He married Deborah Malbone, the daughter of the wealthy merchant Godfrey Malbone. Their sixth child, William, became a United States Senator from Rhode Island.

## ART, ARCHITECTURE AND MUSIC

In the field of art, John Smibert, who came to Newport with Berkeley in 1729, responded to an increasing demand for portraits as leading merchants, lawyers and civic leaders wished to have themselves and their families immortalized for posterity in a fashion fitting their growing status. Robert Feke, born in Oyster Bay, Long Island, also received a number of portrait commissions in Newport. Both of these early Newport artists had strong influence on later American portrait painters. There were many other artists who worked in Newport during this period and, if they were less skilled than Smibert and Feke, they nevertheless preserved the likenesses of many Newport residents. Examples of their work can be seen at the Newport Historical Society and the Redwood Library. Although these "limners" or portrait painters did not remain long in one city, several others moved into Newport for short periods before moving on for new commissions. Joseph Blackburn (active 1753-1763) was followed by Gilbert Stuart, Washington Alston and Michele Felice Corné, together with Samuel King and Charles Bird King, who worked in the post-Revolution and Federal periods. The miniaturist Edward Greene Malbone was a Newporter whose work was also greatly prized.

Newport experienced a remarkable flowering in architecture as well during this period, and at least 214 of the buildings erected still stand today. Unlike earlier periods, when houses were built either by their owners or by anonymous "housewrights," by the mid-18th century master builders and architects began to design buildings following the latest styles popular in England and Europe. Richard Munday's Trinity Church (1726), Seventh Day Baptist Meeting House (1729) and the Colony House (1736-39) are lasting monuments to his taste and skill. Munday was a master builder and was influenced in a general way by Christopher Wren, the English architect who gained international reputation for his work rebuilding London after the Great Fire in 1666. Munday's buildings are in the Georgian, or English Baroque, style.

Peter Harrison, who followed Munday as the chosen designer of important public buildings, worked in a very different style. Often described as America's first architect, Harrison, a merchant by trade, designed the Redwood Library (1748), Touro Synagogue (1763) and the Brick Market (1762-72) in Newport, as well as Christ Chapel in Cambridge and King's Chapel in Boston. He amassed a library of books on architecture that was impressive by colonial standards. Many of these works contained drawings that illustrated the latest English fascination with Roman and Greek antiquity, and it was here that he found inspiration for many of his buildings. He was the first true interpreter in America of the work of Italian Renaissance architect Andrea Palladio, and the classical influence on his buildings, which seemed almost avant garde when first constructed, is most apparent in Redwood Library and the Brick Market.

The world of music in Newport was enriched with Bishop George Berkeley's gift of an organ to Trinity Church in 1733. The *Mercury* carried advertisements saying that William Selby, organist "just arrived from London . . .would instruct young Gentlemen and Ladies to play upon the violin, flute, harpsichord, guitar, and other instruments." Concerts by Boston musicians were not infrequent and private concerts could be arranged with Henry Hymes for a fee.

*Three buildings designed by Richard Munday. Trinity Church (1726), The Seventh Day Baptist Meeting House (1729) and the Colony House (1736-39). The Seventh Day Baptist Meeting House is attached to the Newport Historical Society, and it shows Munday's skill as a designer and the virtuosic techniques of his wood-workers.* NHS P674, P675, P579.

Dancing was a favorite form of amusement. As early as 1745 thirteen local bachelors formed an Assembly and issued invitations to thirty-two "qualified young ladies." Dancing schools increased and French dancing masters advertised. Dinners were often followed by dancing as well as cards, backgammon and billiards. "Turtle Frolics" were very popular as a summer entertainment. Jahleel Brenton's slave "Cuffee Cockroach" was always in great demand as a turtle cook. These frolics were usually held on Goat Island near Fort George and went on from early afternoon until they closed with a hot toddy about midnight.

## EARLY SUMMER VISITORS

During this period Newport began to receive its first "summer visitors." The prosperity, culture, "salubrious climate" and accessibility by sea drew summer colonists from the West Indies, Charleston, South Carolina, and Philadelphia. A few came from England, Scotland, Ireland and the continent to enjoy Newport as a famous "watering place." They followed in the footsteps of the Narragansett Indians who, before European settlement, came over from the mainland during the summer.

Planters from South Carolina discovered Newport as a refreshing haven from the heat, disease and threat of slave insurrections they faced in the south. The "First Families" of South Carolina who came as summer visitors included the Izards, Manigaults and Middletons: those from Philadelphia included the Whartons, Biddles, Nichols, Rawles and Mifflins.

The enterprising Samuel Hall and his successor Solomon Southwick at the *Newport Mercury* were the first journalists in America to introduce a "Society" column. In addition to the commercial news of ship arrivals and departures, the *Mercury* included a list of summer visitors arriving or leaving for the Season, May through October. From 1767 until hostilities began in 1776, the *Mercury* carried this "social register" as a popular feature.

In the first two decades of this golden age many of the streets of Newport were paved, making them superior to those of both Charleston and Philadelphia. A lottery was held to raise money to pave Thames and the Parade, now Washington Square, and this proved so successful that this method was used to fund paving in other parts of the city as well.

## NEWPORT CRAFTSMEN

A large class of Newport artisans and craftsmen producing goods for consumption both in Newport and abroad was one of the reasons the city was prospering. Historians estimate that in the 1760s 99 cabinet-makers, 17 chairmakers and 2 upholsterers plied their trade in Newport. Other woodworkers included 4 carvers, 1 turner and 16 joiners who may have worked on furniture, ships and buildings. The early silversmiths, Arnold Collins, Samuel Vernon, Benjamin Brenton, John Coddington and Daniel Russell, worked early in the 18th century, while John Tanner, Jonathan Otis, Walter Cornell, Nicholas Geoffroy and William Nichols worked late in the 18th century and into the 19th, surviving the lean Federal Period in Newport. The great clockmaking family of William and Thomas Claggett, along with James Wady, flourished during most of the 18th century. High prices for Claggett clocks today do not mean that their maker prospered. Thomas Claggett died a pauper. His coffin was made by Job Townsend II for $2 from the poor fund.

*Parliament clock by William Claggett, ca. 1743. This clock was installed in the Seventh Day Baptist Meeting House. Claggett was one of the first Newport clockmakers to machine his own clock works, and in newspapers of the period he was also described as a "brass founder."* NHS collection.

*Job Townsend's account book, in the collection of the Newport Historical Society, lists a number of pieces of furniture made for Matthew Cozzens. This fine Queen Anne style bookcase on desk, or "secretary," was probably one of them.* NHS78.3.

The best known Newport craftsmen were members of the Town-send and Goddard families, whose cabinets and chairs, clock cases and other furniture have few if any superiors in taste and beauty. Job Townsend (1699-1765) and his brother Christopher started the family cabinetmaking business. Job's daughter Hannah married John Goddard (1732-1783) and three of their fifteen children became excellent cabinet-makers. In all, there were eight Townsends and six Goddards who were master craftsmen. This trade carried over into the 19th century but could not survive the depressed post-Revolution economy of Newport. Much of the furniture made in Newport during this period was made for installation on ships that were built here, shipment into the inland interior, or export via the inter-colonial coastal trade. The rest graced Newport houses, and some local families have owned either Townsend or Goddard pieces for more than two centuries. The furni-ture, like the houses, has survived both the good and bad times. A John Goddard desk and bookcase (known in modern parlance as a "secretary") belonging to the Brown family of Newport and Providence was sold for 12.5 million dollars at auction in 1989.

Most of the artisans who lived in Newport were supplying an enor-mous range of products to a large segment of the population, not just to the wealthy merchant class. Many made the move from artisan to captain to merchant, and some went back again as well. The eve of revolution found most who lived in Newport in opposition to the enforcement of the British Navigation Acts but still basking in comfort and prosperity. With its intellectual attainment, culture, refinement and prosperity Newport had become a genteel, cosmopolitan city.

*Isaac Stelle (1714-1763) painted by Robert Feke. Stelle was a successful ship owner and merchant. In 1761 Stelle joined with prominent merchants of Newport and Providence such as Aaron Lopez, Thomas Robinson, Nicholas Brown and others in the "United Company of Spermaceti Chandlers." These firms made candles from the oil of sperm whales.* NHS25.1.2.

# 3

# The Road to Revolution, Economic Disaster and Revival 1770-1840

The Revolution dealt a crushing blow to the patriotic and militant citizens of Newport. Years before the Declaration of Independence and Revolutionary War, angry seamen and merchants defied the mighty Royal Navy and His Majesty's tax collectors. England's policy changed from looking the other way, in a policy of "benign neglect" when its Navigation Acts were violated, to strict enforcement, with guns if necessary. The war with France which ended with the Peace of Paris in 1763 put a severe strain on the British exchequer, and new ways of raising taxes had to be found. Enforcement of the trade laws in Newport, unfortunately, led eventually to resistance, then revolt, occupation and economic depression.

Adding to the economic and political strain, internal tensions over disagreements about the proper role for Newport in the British imperial system began to divide Newporters. A group of residents known as the "Newport Junto," headed by Dr. Thomas Moffat, Martin Howard, Jr., and some of their Anglican friends, wrote pamphlets and letters to the newspaper openly advocating the creation of a "nobility appointed by the King for life," as well as making major changes in the Rhode Island charter.

## GROWING TENSION WITH BRITAIN

In the French-Indian War of the 1750s, Rhode Island merchants traded with the enemy, especially in the French West Indies. This and other violations of English mercantile regulations throughout the colonies led England to enforce existing trade laws and pass others such as the Stamp Act of 1765, which levied a tax on all legal documents. This tax affected every business transaction, and anger arose among the citizens of Newport over this added burden. Liberty and trade were the paramount issues. In 1764 HMS *Squirrel* prevented a Newport armed vessel from recapturing a colonial brig caught smuggling. A British officer landing from a boat at Malbone's Wharf was seized by the mob and the boat's crew stoned. During the following summer HMS *Maidstone* was impressing seamen in Newport Harbor. A press gang took the entire crew of one brig, but a mob seized the press gang's boat, dragged it to the Parade, and burned it. Tempers, therefore, were already running high when the Stamp Act was passed.

Dr. Moffat, Martin Howard, Jr., and Augustus Johnston, the Stamp Act agent, were burnt in effigy on the Parade during this period of high tension. The following evening a vicious mob, inflamed by "strong drink in plenty with Cheshire cheese and other provocatives to intemperance and riot," first attacked and then sacked Howard's house (now known as the Wanton-Lyman-Hazard House), then Moffat's, and finally forced the otherwise popular Johnston to resign his odious position. "Liberty" was the excuse given for mob action under the direction of Samuel Vernon, William Ellery and others of the local gentry. In the winter of 1766 a large butternut tree standing at the north end of Thames Street was dedicated as the "Tree of Liberty," set apart for the Sons of Liberty to use as a monument to their noble opposition to the Stamp Act. Its beautiful successor remains today close to the same spot.

The crisis deepened when radical patriots in Providence burned the revenue schooner *Gaspee* in 1772 and the Royal Navy made a show of strength in Newport Harbor. Newport's long-standing reputation for lawlessness was catching up with it, and a group of worried conservative merchants made a plea for a return to law and order. Newport's frustration in trying to survive within the restricted trade policy of the mother country was growing.

Three years after the *Gaspee* incident, Captain James Wallace in command of His Majesty's Frigate *Rose* arrived off Newport, her mission to curb smuggling. The *Rose* threatened Newport, demanding the provision of livestock and other supplies, by force if necessary. Instead of bombarding Newport, however, Wallace raided the

*The Newport Stamp Act riot of 1765 followed rituals of rebellion of long standing in English culture. This detail of a cartoon by Paul Revere, "A View of the Year 1765," shows how hanging political opponents in effigy by a carefully controlled mob was an important part of English rebellious behavior.* Courtesy of the American Antiquarian Society.

nearby communities of Bristol, Jamestown, Block Island, Stonington and New London. The Assembly ordered the removal of the cannon and gunpowder from Fort George on Goat Island and they established Rhode Island's own navy, consisting of the sloop *Katy*, commanded by Abraham Whipple. *Katy* completed the removal of the guns and soon afterwards was renamed *Providence* and transferred to the Continental Navy, established on October 13, 1775, through a resolution introduced in the Continental Congress by Rhode Islander Stephen Hopkins. Esek Hopkins was made Commander-in-Chief, William Ellery was appointed to the Marine Committee in Congress, and Stephen Hazard took command of the *Providence* when Abraham Whipple was given a larger ship in the new fleet. In May 1776 Hazard was relieved for poor performance and John Paul Jones assumed command of the ship.

This growing tension and frustration led the Colony of Rhode Island and Providence Plantations, long a leader in disregard for British authority, to become the first colony in North America to renounce allegiance to the British Crown on May 4th, 1776, declaring:

> . . . Whereas George the Third . . . forgetting his dignity . . . instead of protecting is endeavoring to destroy the good people of this colony . . . by sending Fleets and Armies to America to confiscate our property and spread Fire Sword and Desolation throughout our Country . . .

## BRITISH OCCUPATION AND THE BATTLE OF RHODE ISLAND

Two months later Stephen Hopkins of Providence and William Ellery of Newport signed the Declaration passed by the Continental Congress in Philadelphia. This "treason," along with smuggling and destructive acts against the Royal Navy, put Newport in a still more precarious position. In December of that year a large army under General Clinton occupied Newport. With a British fleet in the harbor and an army quartered in the city, the population dropped from about 11,000 in 1775 to 5,300 in 1776. Ezra Stiles fled to Dighton, Massachusetts, taking most of his flock with him.

After the French Treaty of Alliance was ratified in 1778 and Holland and Spain joined France as allies, England found herself fighting a major world war. Two months later Admiral d'Estaing arrived off Newport with a large French fleet. The British prepared for a long siege, but Lord Howe damaged some of the French ships in a brief engagement. Both fleets were hit by an August hurricane and dispersed for repairs.

Deprived of French assistance, an American force under General John Sullivan waiting on the outskirts of Newport had to retreat. The Battle of Rhode Island, the only major land engagement in Rhode Island, was fought on 29 August at the northern end of the Island. The patriot army included the First Rhode Island Regiment of the Continental Line, under Colonel Christopher Greene. This unit, which fought in every engagement of the Revolution except two, was desperately under strength at the time of the battle. Indians and Black slaves augmented its ranks, some by arrangement with their owners; others responding to the offer of freedom for serving.

The patriots fought bravely at what is now called "Bloody Brook" in Portsmouth, but could not dislodge the British. They retreated with honor across the Sakonnet to the mainland, where they remained until the British withdrew 14 months later to New York, to shorten their supply lines as part of their new "southern strategy."

During the British occupation Newport's churches were used for barracks or hospitals, but Trinity, the Anglican Church, was spared this humiliation and ruin. The Colony House, which had been used as a barracks and a hospital, was in such bad repair that it had to be boarded up. After the evacuation the Town Meeting had to meet in Touro Synagogue. In October 1779 the departing British forces took the town records with them to New York only to have the ship run aground and founder. The records went down with the ship, but were recovered and stored in wet boxes for three years before being returned to Newport. The damaged fragments were encased in silk and bound in large folio volumes and are now in the collection of the Newport Historical Society.

## THE FRENCH SOJOURN

In the summer of 1780, after the British withdrawal, a large French fleet commanded by Admiral Charles d'Arsac de Ternay landed a large force of five regiments and support troops led by General Rochambeau. The officers and men were welcomed by the few Newporters

*Statue of General Rochambeau, commander of the French forces quartered in Newport during the Revolution. The statue was originally in Equality Park but was later moved to King's Park on the waterfront.* NHS P462.

left. The civilized and proper demeanor of the French (many of them were in fact members of the French nobility) was in marked contrast to the brutality of the British occupation. Rochambeau was quartered in the Vernon house on Clarke and Mary Streets; de Ternay at the Hunter House on Washington Street; de Noailles at Quaker Tom Robinson's just down the street; Duval at the Pitts Head Tavern, which was subsequently moved and is now on Bridge Street; and the brilliant Marquis de Chastellux in the Maudsley house on Spring Street. The colorful Swedish Count Axel von Fersen, who later led the attempt in 1791 to rescue the King and Queen of France, and another of Rochambeau's aides-de-camp, de Damas, were quartered near Rochambeau in Robert Stevens' home on Clarke Street. All of these buildings are well preserved today. Admiral de Ternay died the following winter. His body was buried in a specially consecrated corner of Trinity churchyard. King Louis XVI ordered the monument to his memory that now stands inside Trinity Church.

George Washington visited Newport in March 1781 to meet with Lafayette and Rochambeau to make final plans for the campaign in the South which, it turned out, would win the war. General Nathanael Greene of Rhode Island was having great success wearing down the British in that region. In June 1781 the French left Newport with their American allies for the long march to Yorktown. Washington's army, with the invaluable aid of the French army and navy, forced the surrender of the southern British Army under Cornwallis as a result of that campaign. Another Peace of Paris, this time acknowledging the independence of the United States, was signed two years later.

## INDEPENDENT BUT SHAKEN

By the end of the Revolutionary War, Newport could well have been called a "disaster area." With little or no work available for those left in the city, and uncontrolled inflation of both "continental" and Rhode Island paper money, it was practically impossible to do business. Shipping interests moved to Providence and other ports. Shipyards and ropewalks were quiet. The Redwood Library lost most of its books: Newport citizens had taken them home to "save" them, and the military had taken those on anatomy and medicine. Wharves were neglected and rotting. Warehouses were empty.

Although the Rhode Islanders were known for their militant independence they nevertheless sent delegates to the Continental Congress. This powerless "league of friendship" had no executive or judicial powers and was weak enough so as not to be a threat to that independence, and Rhode Island joined in. Ratifying the Constitution, which replaced the Articles of Confederation and which had much stronger, centralized power, was another matter. The state refused to take part in the Constitutional Convention of 1787 and even rejected the Constitution in a unique popular referendum held the next year. The state had too many supporters of the much maligned but successful system of "paper money" whereby Rhode Islanders had been steadily retiring debt incurred during the Revolution for the state to ratify the new constitution. The "Country Party," which championed the paper money scheme, were also staunch anti-federalists, and they feared that a strong federal government would make them abandon this vastly inflated currency and also pass trade restrictions. They had enough of that from the British. Rhode Island existed as a "foreign nation" until May 29, 1790, when it became the last of the original thirteen colonies to join the Union by ratifying the Constitution.

During John Adams's administration an undeclared war with France was fought on the high seas with some Newporters taking part as privateers. This maritime war did nothing but bring more economic misery to Newport. Providence was well established as the leading port of the State of Rhode Island and Providence Plantations. Its economy was booming while Newport suffered hard times. Impressment of American seamen led to the "Second War with England," the War of 1812. At first the *Yankee* of Bristol and the *Providence* of Newport (Captain Hopkins) had great success as privateers, but by the war's end in 1815 both were out of action.

*Oliver Hazard Perry, victor of the battle of Lake Erie in the War of 1812, started his career as an officer in the young United States Navy at the age of fourteen by serving in the Rhode Island built frigate* General Greene *commanded by his father. Later his first command was of 12 gunboats in Newport.* NHS P597.

Newporters take pride in the heroic naval victory on Lake Erie by Oliver Hazard Perry, whose family moved to Newport from South County when he was a boy. His father, Christopher, was one of the first captains commissioned in the new United States Navy. Oliver's younger brother, Matthew Calbraith Perry, who was born in Newport, was a leading naval figure in the 1840s and 1850s, and organized and led the expedition to open Japan to western trade in 1854.

As peace came another almost fatal blow struck Newport. The "Great Gale," a hurricane in September 1815, came on a rising high tide. Waterfront property was flooded under several feet of salt water. Wharves and shipping and much inland property were smashed by the fury of the wind and water. No other storm until the hurricane of September 1938 caused as much loss of life and property.

From 1800 to 1840 efforts were made to restore the economic life of Newport. The first bank, The Rhode Island Bank, was established in 1795. Two more were chartered in 1803, The Rhode Island Union and the Newport Bank. The latter, though now merged with the Old Colony Bank of Providence, is still located in its original building on the Parade. Attempts were made by the Champlins and the firm of Gibbs and Channing to compete with Providence. They sent ships to the East Indies and brought back china, gameboards, silks and jade. Others made investments in whaling and the textile industry.

*Matthew Calbraith Perry, Oliver's younger brother, was born in Newport and went on to a distinguished naval career capped by his successful mission to Japan and the negotiation of the treaty which opened that country to trade in 1854.* NHS P157.

# A Portfolio of Seven Architects Working in Newport during the 19th Century

*Newport's history is also written on the landscape in the form of architectural history. Because so much of the early architecture has survived there is a particularly broad range of styles and types of architecture from 1675 to the present. With the coming of the summer colony in the 1840s, a new dimension was added to the architectural heritage of the city when these wealthy new residents began employing the country's finest architects to build their summer cottages. In the pages that follow, seven of these architects are illustrated along with examples of their work in Newport.*

*Richard Upjohn (1802-1878).* Courtesy of the American Architectural Foundation, Prints and Drawings Collection, Washington, D.C.

*"Kingscote," on Bellevue Avenue, built for George Noble Jones in 1841. The drawing is by Upjohn himself. The building is owned by the Preservation Society of Newport County and is open to the public.* Courtesy of the Avery Architectural and Fine Arts Library, Columbia University in the City of New York.

*Richard Morris Hunt (1828-1895),*
*one of the foremost 19th-century*
*American architects. Nowhere is his*
*ability to work in a wide variety of*
*styles over the course of his career*
*more evident than in the buildings*
*he designed in Newport.* Courtesy of
the American Architectural Foundation,
Prints and Drawings Collection,
Washington, D.C.

*Travers Block, at the corner of Bellevue Avenue and Memorial Boulevard, was*
*one of Hunt's first buildings in Newport. Built in the Stick Style ca. 1875, it*
*was designed with shops on the first floor and apartments on the second.* NHS P671.

*"Belcourt Castle," on Bellevue Avenue, was designed for O.H.P. Belmont in 1882. The building reflects Belmont's love of horses and is, in essence, a stable with a house attached. The two large arches in the front were for horse-drawn carriages which could pull inside and unload guests directly into the large hall on the first floor. The building is operated by The Royal Arts Foundation and is open to the public.*
Courtesy of the American Architectural Foundation, Prints and Drawings Collection, Washington, D.C.

*"Marble House," on Bellevue Avenue, was designed for William K. Vanderbilt between 1888 and 1892. This view is from an early postcard. The building is owned by the Preservation Society of Newport County and is open to the public.*
NHS P604.

*George Champlin Mason (1820-1894).
Mason was born in Newport and
was a man of many talents. In addition to designing many early Victorian
buildings, he was author of* Newport
and its Cottages, *served as an editor
for the* Newport Daily News *and
was one of the founders of the
Newport Historical Society in 1853.*
NHS P116.

*George Champlin Mason's drawing of his own house on Sunnyside Place.*
NHS P612.

*Henry Hobson Richardson (1838-1886) was one of the most innovative architects of the period. His designs reflect his interest in early European architecture and the style "Richardsonian Romanesque" was named for him.*
Detail of a photograph courtesy of the Society for the Preservation of New England Antiquities, Boston, Massachusetts.

*Watts Sherman House, on Shepard Avenue, was designed by H. H. Richardson in collaboration with Stanford White in 1874.* NHS P678.

*Robert S. Peabody (1845-1917), of the firm Peabody and Stearns. Less well known than some other architects, Peabody and Stearns nevertheless designed a number of fine buildings in Newport. Frederick Vanderbilt, one of the most independent members of that family, chose Peabody and Stearns to build his house in Newport, "Rough Point," rather than Richard Morris Hunt, who was used by most of the other members of his family for their summer cottages.* Courtesy of the Boston Architectural Center Memorial Library.

*The original "The Breakers," was built 1877-1878 by the Boston firm Peabody and Stearns for tobacco heir Pierre Lorillard. This Queen Anne and Georgian style building was sold in 1885 to Cornelius Vanderbilt II who later commissioned the same firm to make alterations. "The Breakers" burned down in November of 1892 and was subsequently replaced by the now familiar Renaissance Revival palace, designed by Richard Morris Hunt and completed in 1898.* NHS collection.

*Stanford White (1853-1906), of the firm McKim, Mead and White, was a colorful, flamboyant cultural celebrity. He was killed by his lover's jealous husband while sitting in the roof garden restaurant atop the old Madison Square Garden which he himself designed.* Courtesy of the New-York Historical Society.

*Interior view of "Southside," the residence of Robert Goelet on Ochre Point Avenue in 1881-1882. White's artistic genius was often most evident in his interiors.* Courtesy of the New-York Historical Society.

*Horace Trumbauer (1868-1938) worked*
*primarily in the Philadelphia area*
*but designed summer houses in other*
*parts of the country.* Courtesy of
the American Architectural Foundation,
Prints and Drawings Collection,
Washington, D.C.

*"The Elms," on Bellevue Avenue, was built 1900-1902 for Edward J. Berwind.*
*The building was modeled after a chateau seen by the Berwinds while travelling*
*in France. Berwind was an avid gardener and the grounds were landscaped by*
*Ernest Bowditch. The building is owned by the Preservation Society of Newport*
*County and is open to the public.* NHS P605.

Eleven Newport ships were active in whaling. Several steam cotton mills were built, mostly in the wharf area. Even though these mills were kept operating for twenty years or more, neither they nor the whalemen became a strong factor in Newport's economy. The advent of railroads made it possible for the manufacturing towns of Connecticut and Massachusetts to get their products to market in Boston and New York quickly, while Newport had to ship by sea.

## THE RETURN OF SUMMER VISITORS

The Ante-Bellum period witnessed the return and rapid expansion of the summer resort industry so successful in the 18th century. Visitors in the 18th and early 19th century stayed in rooms or houses rented for the season. During the 1830s this pattern began to change. Hotels were built and real estate speculators bought large tracts of land which, in many cases, still remained in the hands of the families who received them as farm lots when the town was first laid out in 1639. The Francis Brinley House on Catherine Street was renamed the Bellevue Hotel in 1825 and opened for business. Its advertisement in 1828 has the sound of affluent luxury. In the 1840s the famed Atlantic House and Ocean House were opened on Bellevue Avenue, and the heyday of Newport's summer hotels began. The Ocean House was destroyed by fire in 1846 but was rebuilt and immediately became a symbol of luxury. Its wide veranda was equipped with comfortable chairs. It boasted a 250-foot corridor and spacious rooms with high ceilings. Every August the hotel was the scene of a magnificent ball for 300 guests who paid $10.00 apiece, a very large sum in that period. Dancing continued until four in the morning.

Other changes came to Newport as summer visitors increased in number. Sail ferries were replaced by steam, and, as early as 1817, the steamboat *Firefly* made the trip from Newport to Providence. Small steamers connected Newport with all the ports of Narragansett Bay. Larger steamers ran to Wickford, Providence and Block Island.

The famed Fall River Line made daily runs between New York, Newport and Fall River, connecting with the railroad to Boston. Starting with the first overnight steamboat, *Bay State*, in 1847, the Fall River Line provided truly luxurious accommodations on magnificent steamboats such as the *Commonwealth* and *Priscilla*. Ninety years later the line was weakened by the Great Depression and the growing reliance on automobiles and trucks. Finally, in 1937, a strike by employees bankrupted the already economically weakened line. But these palatial ships had made the overnight voyage between Newport and New York an experience never to be forgotten.

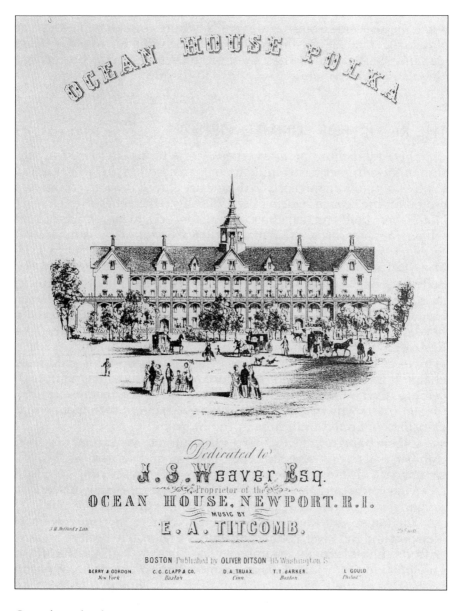

*Cover from the sheet music to "The Ocean House Polka" with an engraving of the hotel from across Bellevue Avenue. The Ocean House, first built in 1840, was Newport's best known hotel. This polka was dedicated to J.S. Weaver, the hotel's proprietor.* NHS collection.

The Narragansett Steamship Co⁰⁵ Steamer **B R I S T O L** of the Fall River Line, Capᵗ A.G. Simmons.

*The* Bristol, *one of the early ships of the New England Steamship Company's Fall River Line. The* Bristol *burned at the docks in Newport in 1888.* Currier and Ives print courtesy of the Rhode Island Historical Society.

A favorite of the fashionable society in Newport was the so-called "Queen of the Bay," the side-wheeler *Eolus*, which carried passengers and freight between Wickford and Newport. The *Eolus* was also available for charter. One New Yorker took over the whole vessel for his private use on trips to and from Newport. The fast New Haven and Old Colony Railroad trains from New York stopped at Wickford, where Newport's "elite" with their horses, coaches and baggage transferred to the steamer. At the end of the season the trip would be made in reverse. Weekend commuters preferred the bay voyage to the longer trip via Providence.

All these improvements in transportation were essential to the gradual emergence of Newport as the "Queen of Resorts" in the second half of the 19th century.

*Mrs. William Backhouse Astor (née Schermerhorn) painted by Carolus Duren in Paris in 1890. Mrs. Astor is wearing a gown by Paris designer Worth. The portrait indicates how important French styles were to summer colonists in Newport during the Gilded Age.* Courtesy of Astor's Beechwood, Newport, Rhode Island.

# 4

# Queen of Resorts
# 1840-1930

The era of Newport's great hotels (1830-1860) had a lasting effect on the City's economy and influenced its future. Newport's climate, a remarkable asset, continued to draw wealthy families from the South who joined with the "first families" of Philadelphia, New York, Providence and Boston. They revived the 18th-century colonial custom of summering in Newport. At first they rented houses, then vied with each other to build their own summer "cottages."

## THE FIRST COTTAGES OF THE SUMMER COLONY

The area chosen for this development was on the hill behind the Redwood Library and spread along Kay Street, Catherine Street and Old Beach Road down to Easton's Pond. A new street, Bath Road (now Memorial Boulevard), was laid out to allow easy access to Easton's, or Newport Beach. As early as 1835 the large estate of the Kay family, from which the street draws its name, was bought from Trinity Church by Lieutenant Governor George Engs and laid out for summer cottages. Development extended to adjacent Bellevue Avenue and along Catherine Street.

This residential section was at first dominated by large estates: the Ralph Izard house off Kay Street; "Belair," the home of R. Allen Wright on Old Beach Road; and David Sears' "Red Cross" cottage off Old Beach Road. Below these and overlooking Easton's Pond was the farm of R.M. Gibbs of New York. The farmhouse was once a sports fisherman's retreat. Charlotte Cushman, the actress, built a large Victorian cottage with fronts on both Catherine Street and what is now Rhode Island Avenue which was designed by the architect who, more than any other, shaped architectural style and taste in Newport during the 19th and early 20th centuries — Richard Morris Hunt. In 1871 Hunt also designed "Linden Gate" for Henry Marquand at Rhode Island Avenue and Old Beach Road, surrounded by spacious grounds, beautiful trees and a low brick wall. It was, unfortunately, lost to a fire in February of 1973. There were at least three other private residences designed by Hunt in this area of Newport, but they have all been either destroyed or torn down.

The genteel atmosphere drew residents to the area who were among the intellectual elite of the nation. Katherine Prescott Wormeley, noted for her translations of French literary classics and her service in the Sanitary Commission during the Civil War, left a manuscript, now in the Redwood Library, describing her Newport. It lists two dozen distinguished families who "formed the winter colony of Newport through the fifties." Throughout the 19th century one could expect to meet in Newport noted scientists, lawyers, statesmen, artists and patrons of art, philanthropists, stage celebrities, novelists, historians and physicians.

*"Red Cross," on Old Beach Road, designed by Richard Morris Hunt for C.J. Peterson ca. 1872. This house, now demolished, was one of many residences designed by Hunt in this neighborhood in that decade.* From Newport and its Cottages, by George Champlin Mason.

At the rumble of war in the late 1850s, Southern families like the Izards failed to return, but the city was on the move after a long period of suspended animation. This was largely due to the work of land speculators, especially Alfred Smith and his associate Joseph Bailey. Smith was a native Newporter who made a fortune as a tailor in New York City and returned to double it in real estate. He opened up the hill behind the Redwood Library and laid out Bellevue Avenue south to Bailey's Beach, creating large tracts of land for subdivision and sale. This development resulted in residential areas characterized by streets lined with well-kept lawns and arched by shade trees, considered the most beautiful in all New England. Many of these trees were imported specimens. For instance, one may see in one block many species of beech trees; standard, copper, weeping and fern-leaf.

Throughout Newport these changes produced an extraordinary building boom. Much of the Kay-Catherine-Old Beach area had remained rural until the 1870s. From 1870 to 1883 more than sixty new houses were built in this area alone. The smaller lots on which these summer homes were built made a very different scene from that on southern Bellevue Avenue where extensive grounds surrounded the palatial homes.

This development laid the base for Newport's emerging in the post-Civil War era as the premier "cottage resort," more distinguished than those like Saratoga Springs which continued to revolve around hotel life. "The Queen of Resorts" was fast becoming the summer capital of the nation's high society. The Gilded Age had arrived.

## THE GILDED AGE

Unlike the more relaxed atmosphere before the Civil War, the Gilded Age was a time of anxious competition among the wealthiest families in the nation. The name for the period originated with the title of a novel written by Mark Twain and Charles Dudley Warner in 1873 satirizing the excesses of the time. Many fought desperately to gain entrance to those inner circles of exclusivity described by Ward McAllister's famous phrase "the 400." The phrase originated because Mrs. William Backhouse Astor's ballroom in her New York City town house could accommodate only 400 guests. As the Astors, the Vanderbilts, the Belmonts and others began summering in Newport, they brought their polite battles for social standing with them.

The goal was to look as much like European aristocracy as possible, and this new generation of summer colonists employed some of the nation's best young architects such as Richard Upjohn, Richard Morris Hunt, H.H. Richardson, Horace Trumbauer and the firms of McKim, Mead, & White, and Peabody and Stearns, as well as local architects like George Champlin Mason and Dudley Newton to build the costly summer villas in the latest French and Italian styles in the more grandiose section of town. The results were the mansions for which Newport has become so famous: "Kingscote," "Chateau-Sûr-Mer," "The Elms," "Rosecliff," "Marble House," "Belcourt Castle," "Ochre Court," "Southside," "Beechwood" and, of course, "The Breakers."

These extravagant monuments to the wealth and taste of their owners were designed as summer pavilions for the rituals of conspicuous consumption so important for the social status of the families of the summer colony. The buildings themselves remain as yet another chapter in the stunning architectural heritage of Newport. Not only does Newport have the largest number of pre-Revolutionary buildings in North America, it also has some of the most important architectural efforts of these young men who together in Newport helped forge an American school of architecture.

Naturally, with a steady influx of visitors and residents who combined wealth and a taste for social intercourse, clubs and cultural societies multiplied. Many older ones fell by the wayside because of changing fashion, but several chartered during the last half of the 19th century have prospered. The Newport Historical Society was organized in 1853 and chartered the following year. Dr. David King was its first president. It already existed as the "Southern Cabinet" of the Rhode Island Historical Society, with the "Northern Cabinet" in Providence.

The Newport Reading Room was also incorporated in 1853. A men's social club, it has occupied its original clubhouse since that year, making it the oldest men's club in America still in its original location. Many distinguished gentlemen have passed through its doors. The best known incident at the Reading Room involved an English polo player, Captain Candy, and his host, the flamboyant James Gordon Bennett, Jr. Candy, encouraged by Bennett, agreed to ride his horse up the steps and into the clubhouse. This led to Candy's expulsion and Bennett's resignation. Bennett, for revenge, founded a rival social club, The Newport Casino, in 1880, which today houses the Tennis Hall of Fame. The Newport Country Club, noted for its golf facilities, was formed fourteen years later. The club was one of the five charter members of the United States Golf Association.

In 1873 Newporters and summer visitors recognized a need for a hospital in which to treat sick and injured sailors as well as their own illnesses, and the Summer Colony held a number of benefits to raise money for its construction. Henry Ledyard, the president, and

*The interior of the Seventh Day Baptist Meeting House when it was used as the museum of the Newport Historical Society. In the center is the model for the statue of Oliver Hazard Perry in Eisenhower Park.* NHS P650.

*The Newport Reading Room on Bellevue Avenue ca. 1910 with an electric car parked in front.* NHS P90.

the board of trustees hired a former Civil War nurse as superintendent and collected a medical board, or staff, of six doctors, all of whom
were graduates of recognized medical schools. When the wooden
building on Friendship Street opened to receive patients in October
1873 it was one of the first three hundred hospitals in the country.

The Spouting Rock Beach Association, popularly known as
"Bailey's Beach," incorporated as a club in 1897, was originally a part
of Alfred Smith's development of Bellevue Avenue. Landowners who
bought a lot from Smith received a "cabana" at Bailey's Beach as part
of the deal. Gradually those families who received rights to use
"Bailey's" gave up the fashionable Easton's, or Newport Beach, where
ladies had to retire at noon so that the gentlemen could bathe in the
nude. Newport Beach continued to be popular with the year-round
residents and day-visitors to Newport until the 1938 hurricane
destroyed the roller coaster, dance halls, carrousels and other amuse-
ments which had been built there.

*Joe Forbes and Emily Willis at Bailey's Beach ca. 1905. The photograph was
taken by Henry O. Havemeyer, one of the most avid photographers among the
summer colonists.* NHS P619.

The Clambake Club of Newport on Easton's Point in Middletown, founded as a gentlemen's fishing club at about the same time as Spouting Rock Beach Association, continues as a private club. It is noted for the excellent seafood in its restaurant. The present clubhouse replaced one washed away in the 1938 hurricane.

The Newport Art Museum and Association, chartered in 1912, is located in the J.N.A. Griswold House, designed by Richard Morris Hunt about 1862. Its grounds on Bellevue Avenue opposite Touro Park complement the trees and shrubs of the Redwood Library. The Cushing Art Gallery is located within these grounds.

## YACHTING IN NEWPORT

Yachting also grew in popularity during this period and, with the arrival in 1883 of the New York Yacht Club's annual regatta, Newport was thrust into the yachting spotlight. This annual event brought yachts from New York up to Newport and then further up the coast. In 1890, after adding Newport as one of its official stops along the way, the club opened Station No. 6 in what is now The Moorings restaurant at the end of Sayer's Wharf. As interest in the sport burgeoned, two local clubs were also formed — the Newport Yacht Club in 1893 and the Ida Lewis Yacht Club in 1928. The former has always drawn more year-round residents and the latter more members of the summer colony. In 1945 the New York Yacht Club sold its facility on Sayer's Wharf and moved its station to the Ida Lewis Yacht Club.

The Ida Lewis Yacht Club was started in 1928 at the Lime Rock Lighthouse. Ida Lewis was the daughter of the Lime Rock Light keeper, and took over his duties when he suffered a stroke. She became nationally famous for her skill and courage in saving at least 18 lives of accident victims from the waters of Newport Harbor. Soon after her death the light was automated, the lighthouse on Lime Rock was connected to shore by a pier, and the Club was formed. The Ida Lewis Yacht Club burgee consists of a red background with a blue symbolic lighthouse and eighteen white stars which represent the lives saved by Newport's equivalent of England's heroine, Grace Darling.

The tiny lighthouse, now the clubhouse, has been the center of an impressive number of international yachting events, such as the America's Cup Defenses, the Newport-to-Bermuda and Annapolis-to-Newport races and the World Championship of the One Ton Ocean Racers from around the world. The club's first commodore was Arthur Curtiss James, owner of a large estate in Newport and a magnificent yacht, the bark *Aloha*. The *Aloha* was equipped with auxiliary power. She had a berth in New York as well as in Newport. Her owner had

*Idawalley Zorada Lewis, the daughter of the Lime Rock Lighthouse keeper, who became a household name for her daring rescues in Newport Harbor.* NHS P648.

*The former Lime Rock Lighthouse where Ida Lewis and her family lived. The light-house is now the home of the Ida Lewis Yacht Club and is connected to the shore by a causeway.* NHS P649.

*Arthur Curtiss James'*
Aloha *tied up in Newport.*
*Her figurehead was modeled*
*after an Hawaiian Queen,*
*Liliuokalani.* NHS P587.

cruised more than 200,000 miles in his earlier yachts and topped it off with a round-the-world cruise in 1921. Between cruises to exotic ports, *Aloha* could be seen on weekends in Long Island Sound, bringing owner and guests to and from Newport, under full sail if conditions permitted. She was such a big ship and such a constant visitor that she employed many more Newporters than other similar ships. There are still stories that circulate in Newport families about a grandfather or an uncle who served in the *Aloha*.

The annual cruise of the New York Yacht Club brought many great yachts to the harbor, such as the three *Corsairs* of J.P. Morgan and his son Jack; Mrs. Marjorie Post Hutton's *Sea Cloud*; Gerald Lambert's record-breaking tall three-masted schooner *Atlantic*; Mrs. Emily Roebling Cadwallader's *Savarona II*; Henry Manville's *Hi-Esmaro*; John Jacob and Vincent Astor's *Nourmahal*; James Gordon Bennett's *Lysistrata* and the luxury yachts of the various Vanderbilts.

## THE CIVIL WAR: THE NAVY COMES TO NEWPORT

In the midst of this seemingly endless string of calm gay summers filled with sports, entertainments in houses resplendent with valiant efforts to impress and year-round residents struggling to make enough money during the season to tide them over the rest of the year, the threat of the Civil War clouded the horizon. Ironically, Newport had always enjoyed a close bond with the South and there was a strong southern social atmosphere. Southerners owned property, married and died in Newport. It was a surprise, therefore, to the South when Newport strongly opposed secession and made ready for war.

Stirring patriotic parades, fireworks and salutes by the Newport Artillery Company marked Washington's birthday and the inauguration of Lincoln in February and March, 1861. The Artillery Company was chartered by George II in 1741 and is the oldest military unit in America operating under its original charter. Its headquarters are still in the stone armory on Clarke Street, and its members were staunch supporters of the Union. In April came the news that Fort Sumter had been attacked, followed by the president's call for 75,000 volunteers. Almost all the members of the Artillery Company volunteered and in one day Newport's quota was filled. The contingent was ordered to Providence to join the First Rhode Island Regiment. On April 17th an enthusiastic but tearful following escorted these men to the steamer *Perry*. They were soon joined by the Second Rhode Island Regiment with 130 Newporters serving in Companies "F" and "K." In July they marched bravely into Virginia with colors flying but were routed at Bull Run.

As the casualty lists were published the horrors of war were brought home to families, friends and sweethearts. As the war progressed, the Sanitary Commission established a hospital at the former Portsmouth Grove Recreation Center, now called Melville. Newport's Kate Prescott Wormeley, fresh from service with the Commission on the battlefield, became "Lady Superintendent" of this hospital. Miss Wormeley, a truly remarkable woman with enormous energy, employed poor women of Newport during the first part of the war, making shirts for the Army. After the war Miss Wormeley founded a vocational school on Broadway which became the Townsend Industrial School and then, later, the Thompson Junior High School. In 1886 she also founded an organization which was the precursor of today's Visiting Nurse Service of Newport County.

The Civil War had another profound effect on Newport — it officially brought the Navy to Newport for the first time. Soon after the Battle of Bull Run the Naval Academy was moved to Newport from Annapolis. It occupied the Atlantic House Hotel facing Touro Park

*U.S. Naval Academy midshipmen in front of the Atlantic House Hotel across from Touro Park ca. 1862. The Naval Academy was moved to Newport during the Civil War.* NHS P167.

at Bellevue Avenue and Pelham Street. "Old Ironsides," the USS *Constitution*, was also used to house midshipmen for training. Among other ships used for training was the famous yacht *America*. Touro Park made an excellent drill ground. Although the academy remained for only four years, the Navy gradually became an integral part of the city's life.

The war over, the Naval Academy returned to Annapolis, but the Navy was in Newport to stay. In 1869 Goat Island with its old fort was equipped with piers and a laboratory and factory for the manufacture and testing of torpedoes and other new weapons, and the Naval Torpedo Station was born. Primarily concerned with research and development until the 1930s, the growing threat of World War II brought drastic increases in the productive capacity of the facility. At its peak in the mid-1940s, the Torpedo Station employed more than 14,000 Newporters, making it the only large industrial plant ever to operate in Newport.

*Rear Admiral Stephen B. Luce, who established the Naval Training Station in Newport in 1883 and the Naval War College in 1884.* NHS P162.

In 1883 Commodore Stephen B. Luce established the Naval Training Station on Coaster's Harbor Island. This was the forerunner of the modern recruit training stations for enlisted men in the Navy. Before the Training Station was founded, navy recruits received no formal education or training but learned their trade at sea in ships. In 1884 Luce established the Naval War College in the building which once housed the "Deaf and Dumb Asylum" (Newport's name for its poorhouse), now Founders Hall and the site of the Naval War College Museum.

The War College quickly became the U.S. Navy's premier institution for professional thinking about warfare, international law and statesmanship relating to war and peace. Among others, Luce brought to the College Captain Alfred Thayer Mahan, the naval historian whose monumental book *The Influence of Sea Power Upon History, 1660-1783* and other works influenced naval thought around the world. In 1887 the first naval war games were played at the War College. This innovation, along with high academic standards, brought a new level of sophistication to professional, graduate education for senior officers in the Navy and other branches of the service. In addition to creating and maintaining a prestigious graduate school, Luce and Mahan, and the many others who have come to the Naval War College to teach and study over the years have played an active part in the social and cultural life of the city.

Newport Harbor and Narragansett Bay have always been safe and deep havens for naval as well as commercial shipping, and their defense has always been a high priority of civilians and military alike. Fort Adams was built in the 1820s as part of a network of coastal

*Aerial view of Fort Adams. The fort was built in the 1820s on the site of an earlier fortification on a point of land that naturally protects Newport's harbor.* NHS P684.

defenses set up under the Jefferson administration, which had been stung by the embargoes of the War of 1812. When the Navy came to Newport after the Civil War, the Fort took on a new significance. Throughout its history until it was closed after World War II it was an Army garrison, usually of regimental strength. Another interesting part of the defenses of Narragansett Bay was the system of great anti-submarine chain nets. Specially designed boats tended the nets and opened and closed the gates.

Shortly after the Civil War the establishment of the Naval Torpedo Station on Goat Island brought a permanent naval presence to Newport. Before World War II Narragansett Bay was used by the fleet only in summertime. The extensive buildup that accompanied that war provided the training facilities and other elements necessary for basing ships here.

## TRANSPORTATION IN THE 19TH CENTURY

In this period permanent Navy facilities and the growing ranks of summer visitors brought a need for more transportation. While most New England communities had railroad services well before the Civil War, Newport did not until the New Haven and Old Colony Railroad, over the objections of Fall River merchants, brought a spur line across the Sakonnet River Bridge and down Aquidneck Island to Newport in 1863. Newport did, however, pioneer in an electric trolley system, starting service in 1889. The trolley ran from the Post Office near the car barn on Commercial Wharf down Bath Road to Easton's Beach and from Two Mile Corner to Morton Park. These trolleys soon replaced horse-drawn omnibuses in many sections of Newport. Interurban trolleys ran the length of the Island and across the Stone Bridge to Tiverton, Fall River, and later, using a ferry to Bristol, through to Providence. At one time it was possible to go by this "light rail" system from Newport through Massachusetts to Nashua, New Hampshire. Newport's trolleys finally, of course, gave way to motor buses. The streetcars made their last run in 1927. The automobile helped replace the Old Colony Railroad, Newport's rail link with the rest of the United States.

With all these new forms of transportation technology, it was still a gorgeous sight to watch "The 400" and other wealthy Newporters drive up and down Bellevue Avenue in their perfectly equipped carriages and four-in-hands. The summer colony tried hard to keep Bellevue Avenue from being paved, but the City Council decided to pass the decision over to the people. A referendum in the early 1920s favored a hard top. By this time automobiles were no longer

*"The Cove" where the Old Colony Railroad line terminated at the New England Steamship Company's Fall River Line docks. The Cove was a tidal basin behind Gravelly Point which was filled in around 1900. Today, The Cove is the site of the Newport County Convention and Visitors Bureau Gateway Center and a hotel.* NHS P679.

sensations and were gradually supplanting the horse and carriage. For those with surplus energy the bicycle became almost a craze during the late 19th century. Long, cross-country cycling trips were organized on the large wheeled "penny farthing" bicycles by the League of American Wheelmen, which was organized in Newport in 1880.

Despite its attachment to horse-drawn carriages, however, the summer colony contributed to the early growth of the automobile industry. Electrics were popular at first, and one defeated a gasoline powered Duryea in the first automobile race in Rhode Island. A parade of 19 electrics took place at Oliver Hazard Perry Belmont's estate "Belcourt." In 1901 William K. Vanderbilt, dubbed "father of automobile racing in America," was victor in the races at Aquidneck Park. Other owner drivers that day included Reginald Vanderbilt, Henry Howard, Mrs. Joseph Widener, the pioneer aviator Hugh L. Willoughby, Mrs. O.H.P. Belmont, Baron de Morogues and O.H.P. Belmont himself.

Faster transportation led to the demand to link Aquidneck Island with the mainland. The Old Stone Bridge, built in the 18th century but blown down by one hurricane after another, was the first bridge to the mainland. The graceful Mount Hope toll bridge between the towns of Portsmouth and Bristol was built during the economic boom of 1928 and opened to travel the following year. This put an end to the Bristol Ferry and made motor travel to and from Newport much more convenient. Two ferry rides were still required on the direct route to New York. Finally, in 1940, Saunderstown and Jamestown were connected by the Jamestown Bridge, which is scheduled to be replaced by 1992. In 1969 the Newport Bridge was completed, connecting Newport with Jamestown while still giving clearance to large vessels. These three and the Portsmouth-Tiverton high bridge, which replaced the Stone Bridge, relieved Newport's dependence on car ferries. The bridges were opposed by a few but cheered by many. They stimulated the development of the entire Island but did away with its often charming insularity.

*Short Line bus company calendar for the year 1929. This calendar was published on the eve of the completion of the Mount Hope Bridge and shows three generations of transportation to Aquidneck Island. Inset on the top is a drawing of the horse-powered ferry which took travelers from Mt. Hope in Bristol to the northern tip of the Island. In the middle was the steam ferry which replaced it. The Mount Hope Bridge pictured on the bottom was in fact completed in that year.* NHS collection.

*Workmen during the restoration of the Cozzens House on Farewell Street.* NHS P593.

CHAPTER

# 5

# Recovery, Restoration and Redevelopment 1930-1976

The Great Depression of the 1930s gradually had its impact on Newport and brought the end of an era. The end of World War II brought the closing of the Torpedo Station and with it the loss of thousands of jobs. The palatial "cottages" of the long-standing summer colony could not easily survive the growing pressure of rising costs and income taxes. Since they generally required large staffs of indoor and outdoor servants they could rarely be used as private year-round homes. The overall change in Newport's status as "Queen of Resorts" was obvious to all.

The business of checking decline by looking for alternatives was slow, painful and marked by wrong turnings and blind alleys, but also by efforts that proved fruitful in the long run. The efforts that proved most successful followed in a long, distinguished tradition of restoring the town's spectacular architectural heritage and finding new uses for older buildings.

## THE PRESERVATION MOVEMENT IN NEWPORT

By the end of World War II, nowhere else in this country was there such an extensive number of buildings covering such a wide period of time, from the late 17th century to the present. The finest examples of every style known in American architecture line the streets of Newport. The survival of so many of these was due to a complex, interrelated set of circumstances. First, unlike almost all the other cities in North America that date to the colonial period, Newport never had the kind of major fire that transformed the landscape of cities like Boston. Second, for a variety of reasons, the pressures of industrialization bypassed Newport. Without an intense demand for housing for the work force in a factory, many of Newport's historic buildings were spared demolition or equally destructive remodelling. Another major factor was that from the mid-1850s Newport self-consciously began to work to preserve these buildings. Much of the impetus for this early preservation thinking came from the intellectuals and architects who began to summer in Newport before the Civil War. Many Newporters, such as George Champlin Mason, his son George, Jr., and Dr. David King, the first president of the Newport Historical Society, also recognized the importance of saving Newport's unique architectural heritage.

What was begun in the 1850s was taken up again in the late 1920s and 1930s. Here again, the Newport Historical Society led the way with its restoration of the Wanton-Lyman-Hazard House, but efforts during this period also included work on the Colony House, Trinity Church and the Brick Market. All these efforts employed the services of architect Norman M. Isham, whose visionary understanding of the importance of sensitive architectural preservation helped make Newport an architectural showcase.

*Preservation architect Norman M. Isham. Isham was involved with the restoration of most of Newport's important colonial buildings: The Wanton-Lyman-Hazard House (1675), Trinity Church (1726), the Colony House (1739), the Brick Market (1762-1772) and others.* Copyright, 1992, used with permission of *The Providence Journal.*

*Mrs. George Henry Warren and John Nicholas Brown. Mrs. Warren helped found the Preservation Society of Newport County. Mr. Brown funded the construction of the chapel at St. George's School and the restoration of the Brick Market in the 1930s.* Photograph copyright John T. Hopf.

The next wave of interest in historic preservation followed after World War II, and the result was one of the great successes in the history of historic preservation in America. During this period many palatial mansions were saved because new uses were found for them, such as housing for a number of private schools. These schools drew many young people to Newport, but, unfortunately, most of these institutions were short lived. On the other hand, Salve Regina University, an accredited college founded in 1947 on Ochre Point by the Catholic Order of the Sisters of Mercy, thrived and expanded and became an academic center. It was either given or purchased a number of the finer late 19th-century buildings in Newport such as "Ochre Court" (designed by Richard Morris Hunt) and the "Watts-Sherman House" (designed by H.H. Richardson and Stanford White). In 1973 Salve became coeducational, and today it offers post-graduate education and includes many part-time students from the Naval War College. The establishment of these schools took some large estates off the tax rolls, but the money spent by these institutions, their faculties and students provides considerable support to the economy of the Island.

The most successful effort to find new uses for Newport's architectural treasures began when a group of summer residents headed by Mrs. George Henry Warren dreamed of a way of saving some

*"The Breakers," Newport's best-known mansion, built for Cornelius Vanderbilt by Richard Morris Hunt between 1892 and 1895. It is now owned by the Preservation Society of Newport County and is open to the public.* NHS P608.

outstanding colonial buildings such as the White Horse Tavern, the Hunter House and also some of the great mansions. The White Horse Tavern is the oldest tavern in the nation and the Hunter House has been named repeatedly as one of the ten outstanding houses in America. Mrs. Warren founded the Preservation Society of Newport County in 1945 and remained its president and guiding spirit for thirty years. The enormous mansion built by Cornelius Vanderbilt II, "The Breakers," now the centerpiece of the Preservation Society's properties, was at first leased to the Society by Vanderbilt's daughter, Countess Laszlo Szechenyi, for one dollar a year and was eventually purchased by the Society.

A large permanent staff at the Preservation Society now maintains, besides "The Breakers" (1895), the Hunter House (1748), the William K. Vanderbilt "Marble House" (1892) and William S. Wetmore's "Chateau-Sur-Mer" (1852) with the elaborate additions by Richard Morris Hunt in 1872. "The Elms," built in 1901 for the coal magnate Edward J. Berwind of Philadelphia, has beautiful grounds which are an impressive sight. Other Preservation Society properties include "Green Animals", the famous topiary gardens in Portsmouth with eighty sculptured trees and shrubs started by Thomas Brayton in 1880, the early Victorian "Kingscote" (1841) and Hermann Oehlrichs' mansion "Rosecliff" (1902).

The popularity of these sites as historic house museums attracts hundreds of thousands of visitors to Newport each year and makes it possible for the Society to bring into the city millions of dollars in tourist money and to provide employment for workers of every description. "The Breakers" alone has had millions of paid visitors.

## SAVING THE COLONIAL CITY

Other organizations have for some years looked to the future through the past. The Newport Historical Society has been a pioneer in preservation and restoration. In 1884 the Newport Historical Society purchased and renovated the beautiful little Seventh Day Baptist Meeting House on Barney Street and moved it in 1887 to the Society's current location on Touro Street. The Society played a pivotal role in the restoration of the Old Colony House after Newport was no longer the joint capital. The Wanton-Lyman-Hazard House (ca. 1675), purchased and restored by the Society in the 1920s, and the Great Friends Meeting House (1699) were additional preservation projects which saved two of Newport's earliest structures. These buildings form

*The Pitts Head Tavern being moved to save it from demolition. Newporters have been moving houses to save them since the 18th century. The unwillingness to let old buildings be torn down is one of the major reasons so much historic architecture has survived in Newport from the 17th century to the present.* NHS P594.

the cornerstone of the city's architectural heritage. The oldest surviving private home in Newport, the Wanton-Lyman-Hazard House, was acquired by the Society and has twice been restored. A more recent restoration has been the Great Friends Meeting House off Marlborough Street. It has been made possible by the foresight, generosity and careful planning of Mrs. Sidney L. Wright and family. After it was restored, the building and its grounds were given to the Historical Society. The building was opened to the public in July 1975 and is also used for the Friends Meeting on two Sundays each month.

In the late 1960s a group of concerned citizens started "Operation Clapboard," and another grass roots preservation movement, which would have far-reaching effects, was underway. Formed by residents of the Point and Historic Hill neighborhoods, where so many colonial and early Victorian buildings stand side by side, this group saw the Preservation Society's efforts begin to concentrate on the later Bellevue Avenue area. Operation Clapboard's plan to save these earlier, more modest buildings was to purchase options on the mortgages of buildings as they came up for sale or were condemned. These options were then sold to individuals (often personally recruited by the members of Operation Clapboard) who were interested in restoring and either living in the buildings, renting them, or selling to someone else.

The success of Operation Clapboard and its offshoot organization, Oldport Association, brought another influential and very powerful force to Newport's effort to make its past support its future: the Newport Restoration Foundation, chartered in 1968. The inspiration came from Doris Duke and Executive Director Francis Adams Comstock. The Foundation has, through careful planning, purchased mostly 18th-century homes and restored them for rent, not sale. Where the bulldozers of "Redevelopment" threatened to tear down, the Newport Restoration Foundation stepped in and bought a colonial house and moved it to a vacant lot purchased for this purpose. The plan for demolition and restoration of the area around Trinity Church, known as Queen Anne Square, was a joint project of the Historic Hill Committee, the Redevelopment Commission, the Newport Restoration Foundation and other groups and individuals. Of course the Newport Restoration Foundation has added greatly to the present and future tax base of the city.

Another preserved historic treasure is "Whitehall," the 1729 home of Dean George Berkeley in the adjoining town of Middletown. It has been restored and is now owned by the National Society of Colonial Dames of America in the State of Rhode Island. In the summer it is open to the public for tours by volunteer and resident guides.

*Thames Street from Washington Square looking north, 1951. The Blue Moon Gardens, whose neon sign is in the foreground, was a notorious night-spot which attracted Navy personnel as well as year-round residents.* Courtesy of Rhode Island Historical Society. RHix32946.

Just as the historic preservation movement was getting underway, redevelopment activity, supported by federal funds, gradually changed the Newport waterfront. In doing so it has opened up a view of the harbor, encouraged investment in new buildings, small businesses linked with tourism and the modernization of large sections of Thames Street. "Redevelopment" has had failures as well as successes. It looked more to the future than to the past for Newport's recovery and may have failed to recognize the serious problem that automobile traffic brings to the area.

All of these changes have not been without cost. The gentrification of many of Newport's neighborhoods through restoration displaced people who had been living there for years. The poorer residents, many of them black, were no longer able to afford to own or rent housing in the downtown area of Newport and have relocated to housing projects, many of which are located on the margins of the city. Now Newport, thought of as a "society" town, has the largest proportion of public housing in the state.

Another significant change in the pattern of Newport history was the decline of the solid summer economy and its gradual replacement by the motoring tourist economy. Spurred by the construction of the Mount Hope, Jamestown and Newport bridges, "day-trippers" began to replace those who stayed for longer periods. The famous beaches of Newport and Middletown are developed to serve large crowds. Caravan campsites have been erected. Areas of the waterfront have become state parks for general recreation. Newport's night life has become a magnet for the young of southern New England.

*Aerial view of Newport waterfront showing the results of redevelopment and the increasing dependence on tourism. America's Cup Avenue, extending along the waterfront, and Memorial Boulevard extending up from the harbor toward Bellevue Avenue are clearly visible. Both these major thoroughfares were cut through existing historic sections to make way for increased automobile traffic.* Courtesy of Tall Ships Newport '92. Photographed by John Byrnes.

*Tall Ship* Libertad *in Newport Harbor with many vessels of the spectator fleet.*
Courtesy of *Newport Daily News*.

CHAPTER

# 6

# Completing Three and a Half Centuries 1976 to Present

As the United States of America celebrated its 200th birthday on the Fourth of July, 1976, Newport looked ahead after its own 337 years with pride, but also with apprehension. As church bells rang and guns boomed around Narragansett Bay's shores that Independence Day, change for the city lay ahead, good for some, disturbing for others. Emphasis within the local economy had started to shift, and the national economy was also changing.

## TOURISM

The three major communities of Newport — year-round residents and businesses, the summer colony, and the Navy and its dependents — have been defined in earlier chapters. By 1976 a fourth community was also well established: tourists, who came in increasing numbers. Tourism brought a changing business structure in the city and on Aquidneck Island. Initially Newport and neighboring towns looked to tourists only to fill the gap in the local economy after Atlantic Fleet units moved away from the area in 1973. In fact, however, most of the city's recent development as well as many of its problems are the result of Newport's extraordinary growth as a tourist attraction of national importance. Funds for development of condominiums, hotels and motels and waterfront changes flowed in from sources outside the city and in many cases outside the state.

Despite Newport's importance to American history from its founding in 1639 and its many historic landmarks of the 17th and 18th centuries, most visitors come to see "The Mansions" — those 19th-

and early 20th-century summer homes along Bellevue Avenue, Cliff Walk and the Ocean Drive. Attendance at the Preservation Society of Newport County's mansions and historic sites grew annually until 1988, when attendance fell off by approximately 6%. More and more use is being made of the mansions for special events, balls and concerts. The acquisition in 1972 of the 1880 house of Miss Alice Brayton, "Green Animals," was a unique addition to the Society. This Victorian era home in Portsmouth, with its topiary gardens near the coastal Old Colony Railroad, is of special interest to children touring with their parents.

The Kennedy "Summer White House," "Hammersmith Farm," the oldest and the last remaining working farm in Newport opened in 1978 as a visitors' attraction. Open for eight months of the year, it has Kennedy memorabilia and a superb location at the entrance of the East Passage. Condominium development of "Harbour Court," the estate of John Nicholas Brown, became a real possibility on his death in 1979 followed by the death of his wife, Ann Kinsolving Brown, five years later. Fortunately, a group of New York Yacht Club members bought the estate from the Brown heirs and established a New York Yacht Club Station, adjacent to the Ida Lewis Yacht Club. In 1988 Station #6 of the New York Yacht Club moved to "Harbour Court", perpetuating the tradition of the original Newport station at Sayer's Wharf.

The Summer Colony, despite the loss of some great estates, continued to thrive. New faces from Texas, Virginia and the western states were added to the social directories and membership rolls of the Spouting Rock Beach Association, the Clambake Club of Newport and the Newport Country Club. At the Country Club, 1980 marked the first annual Senior Pro-Am tournament, which has attracted many of the "greats" of golf to play one of the oldest links in the United States. Tennis has also continued to flourish in several world class tournaments each summer season. The Casino's grass courts hosted players each summer who would find their place soon in the adjacent Tennis Hall of Fame, now firmly established as the shrine of American tennis. As a part of the Casino complex, Newport boasts one of only nine court tennis facilities in the United States. Beginning in 1982 the central grass court of the Casino became the site of croquet tournaments.

Newport became famous for its annual Jazz Festival the first of which was in 1954. Since that date, music festivals have been an important tourist attraction. Unfortunately, the Jazz Festival was discontinued in the 1960s because of what amounted to a riot. In 1981 the Jazz Festival

*Oliver Campbell and Robert Huntington at the conclusion of their singles match in the United States' Lawn Tennis Association's National Championships at the Newport Casino, 1890.* Courtesy of the International Tennis Hall of Fame at the Newport Casino, Newport, Rhode Island.

returned to Newport in the form of gatherings at Fort Adams State Park. Crowd control proved to be far better than twenty years earlier, and the Jazz Festival is once again an annual event, featuring the top jazz soloists and ensembles in the country. In addition, the State Park is the scene of an annual Folk Music Festival, drawing capacity audiences of young people. Newport's Summer Music Festival celebrated its 20th anniversary in 1988 with a gala two-week program. Artists of international fame continue to come here each summer for this nationally acclaimed series of concerts, most of which are held in the mansions of the Preservation Society. Newport's "Concerts on the Island" (COTI) is now in its 20th season of offering winter concerts, while in 1988 the Swanhurst Chorus marked its 60th year. Founded in 1953, the versatile Navy Choristers give five or six concerts each year in support of various Newport charities and non-profit organizations.

*The Jazz Festival in Fort Adams. The Festival started at the Casino, but was temporarily discontinued in the 1960s because of unruly crowds. It has subsequently returned as an annual event to the state park which surrounds Fort Adams.* Photograph copyright John T. Hopf.

Tourism's growth has also brought ever heavier traffic to Newport and Aquidneck Island. Much of the funding for new highways and major repairs has come from state and federal sources. Each summer the streets are congested during maritime events, concerts and tournaments. Shuttle busing from parking areas north of Newport has helped alleviate the problem somewhat. However, Newport's visitors seem to prefer traffic jams to being separated from their vehicles. The 1988 opening of the Newport Gateway, where half a century earlier the New York, New Haven, and Hartford railroad station stood, has provided some additional downtown parking, but is only a small start in solving the overall traffic problem. Operated by the Newport County Visitor and Convention Bureau, it serves as an information center and is helping not only to encourage "heritage" tourism in Newport, but also to organize and direct tourists' visits to the city. Next to the Gateway now stands Newport's newest hotel, the Marriott Hotel.

## YEAR-ROUND RESIDENTS AND THE TOURIST ECONOMY

While real estate development in previous years expanded the city's tax base, costs to the taxpayers grew as a result of tourism. Police and fire services were modernized and a new police station was completed in 1986 near City Hall on Broadway. However, additional manpower remains a serious police requirement when huge crowds of tourists visit the Island each summer weekend.

Newport's mayors in these years, Democrats Humphrey Donnelly, Paul Gaines and Robert McKenna, and Republican Patrick Kirby, have wrestled with tourist related problems. The issues considered by the City Council included modifications of zoning laws to suit hotel and condominium developers, the possibility of legalized gambling in Rhode Island, pressure for more liquor dispensing licenses, and finding ways to make the waterfront still available to commercial fishermen. Too often local decisions were subject to modification by more powerful upstate political factions, who viewed Newport and its adjacent communities only as a source of benefit to the Rhode Island economy as a whole.

*Policeman ticketing cars along Memorial Boulevard during the summer. Since the 1960s, heavy traffic and limited parking are major problems created by the increased flow of tourists into Newport.* Photograph copyright John T. Hopf.

*Sealing the time capsule in front of City Hall as part of Newport's celebration of its 350th anniversary. Officials include many former mayors of Newport. From left to right, bottom row: Fred Alofsin, Robert McKenna; second row: Andrew Hambly, Patrick Kirby, Paul Gaines, H.J. "Harp" Donnelly, David Roderick; third row: Dean Lewis, John Greichen, Harry Winthrop, B. Mitchell Simpson III; top row: Samuel M.C. Barker.* NHS P647.

With the development of more and more condominiums, time-share resorts and other tourist-based businesses on the waterfront to the west of Thames Street, the city's industrial base has been slowly changing as downtown industries closed or relocated. General Electric's plant at the foot of Memorial Boulevard closed in 1978, and the well-built gray stone building was developed with shops and a night club on lower floors and time-share condominiums above. Waterfront shipyards have disappeared from the area except for Newport Offshore at the south end of Washington Street. Newport Electric Corporation has moved its operations from downtown Newport to Middletown.

In 1978 a new shipyard, Derecktor Co., leased former Navy land on Coddington Cove and three years later won a $350 million contract for the construction of nine medium-endurance Coast Guard cutters of the "Bear" class, possibly the largest single contract ever awarded to a Rhode Island firm. Replacing dwindling industries in Newport are the high-tech offices in Middletown and Portsmouth industrial parks, and a steady amount of work at the large Raytheon plant in Portsmouth. The recession of 1991, however, brought lean times for all these industries.

In 1976 the Arthur Curtiss James estate was acquired by New England Properties, Inc., for an alcoholic rehabilitation center, known as Edgehill Newport. The estate at one time or another contained four structures: the house named "Edgehill," a collection of buildings known as "Swiss Village," "Vedimar," which was demolished in 1901, and "Beacon Hill House," which was demolished in 1912. Pushing ahead against objections from many neighboring landowners, the Center opened in 1980 and provided much-needed services with slow expansion of capacity and facilities.

## THE MODERN NAVY IN NARRAGANSETT BAY

Newport's long association with the U.S. military, particularly the United States Navy, has been discussed in previous chapters. Until 1973 the Newport Naval Base was homeport for more than a quarter of the Atlantic Fleet including headquarters of the Cruiser Destroyer Force. By 1971, however, the Nixon Administration had closed the Boston Navy Yard and the Air Station at Quonset Point and moved all but one destroyer squadron to more southern ports. The educational and training facilities remained and the complex which encompassed the Naval Base was renamed the Naval Education and Training Center. The economic impact of these changes was feared by many, but additions to the training complex have partly made up for much of the loss.

The United States Navy continues to play an extremely important part in the Island's economy and in recent years a dozen or more ships have again been homeported in Newport. In addition, a strong Navy presence remained in the form of the Naval Education and Training Center, the Naval War College and the Naval Underwater Systems Center. The budgets of these commands remain a major part of Rhode Island's economy, and the state's delegation in the U.S. Congress worked hard to have facilities modernized and responsibilities increased. Enrollment at the Naval War College increased with the

*Ships of the U.S. Atlantic Fleet moored at Coddington Cove, 1973. Despite the fact that most of the fleet was moved to southern ports starting in 1971, Newport continues to be home port to several ships.* Photograph copyright John T. Hopf.

*Munitions workers at the U.S. Naval Torpedo Station on Goat Island ca. 1943.* NHS P164.

addition of short courses and an enlarged war gaming computer complex. The Destroyer School, redesignated the Surface Warfare School in 1975, trebled its enrollment with more than 1500 student officers taking courses each year. The Naval Academy Preparatory School, with more than 200 prospective midshipmen, was moved to Newport in 1974, although this addition was offset by the closing of the century-old Marine Barracks in 1977.

Surplus Navy land and facilities have been transferred to the Island communities for recreational and educational purposes and to private industry for boat and shipbuilding. Goat Island, forming the west side of Newport harbor, was declared surplus in 1955 after the Naval Torpedo Station was disestablished and joined with the Underwater Systems Center. Today Goat Island is privately owned and developed with a convention center at the Newport Islander Doubletree Hotel (formerly the Sheraton Islander Inn and before that the Hilton Colonial) and an extensive condominium complex. The old Navy piers were modernized into a large berthing area for yachts. Except for the hotel, all rental properties on the Island have been changed to condominium status, a move most dismaying to many tenants who could not afford the cost of purchase.

Rose Island, to the north of Goat Island and previously a storage site for the high explosives used in torpedo manufacture, was also declared surplus. In 1969 it was purchased by developers who planned to construct a condominium complex with adjacent marina. Little support for development was apparent, and there was active opposition from the Rose Island Lighthouse Foundation, a group of dedicated preservationists, as well as residents of the Point section of Newport. The Foundation was successful in obtaining a segment of Rose Island surrounding the lighthouse to be developed as a small park, while restoration began on the century-old structure, which is a National Historic Landmark.

The government's largest industrial complex in Rhode Island, the Naval Underwater Systems Center (NUSC), successor to the former Naval Torpedo Station on Goat Island, continued to expand and brought contractors and engineers from a number of electronic and ordnance companies, most of whom established offices in Middletown and Portsmouth. This influx of relatively high-income families to the area contributed to a rapid increase in real estate values. In 1991 the Navy announced that it would be consolidating the many NUSC facilities throughout the country into four regional centers, and the Newport/Middletown complex was selected to be the center for New England.

*Rose Island Lighthouse, owned by the Rose Island Lighthouse Foundation. Rose Island, the small island visible from the Newport Bridge, is the site of Revolutionary War period British, French and American fortifications.* Courtesy Rose Island Lighthouse Foundation.

Commencing in 1980, as the Navy began a major buildup towards a 600-ship fleet, Newport seemed a likely port to receive additional ships. The immediate benefit for the economy of having more ships homeported here was counterbalanced by the lack of housing and services to support more families, many with low income. Reconstruction of some of the government housing in nearby Middletown helped, but the overall problem of reasonable housing, not just for the Navy but for all of Newport County's low-income residents, is far from solved.

## CELEBRATING THE CITY'S PAST

By 1976 Rhode Island, "The Ocean State," had established a program to help celebrate the nation's Bicentennial. It was fitting that the preliminaries to the great Operation Sail and Naval Review in New York on July 4th took place in Newport and Narragansett Bay. During the last week of June Newport played host to more than twenty of the large Tall Ships and a number of smaller ones with crews from 16 nations. Of particular interest were the two Tall Ships from the USSR, moored off Jamestown and later at Pier 2 in Coddington Cove. On July 1 all these ships sailed out of the Bay in a splendid parade heading south for Operation Sail in New York. Their week in Newport marked the city's greatest traffic-tourist jam with more than 400,000 coming to see the ships. On the day of the departure alone more than 100,000 crowded the shoreline on both sides of the Bay's East Passage.

Ten days later Newport welcomed Britain's Queen Elizabeth and her consort Prince Philip on a brief visit to the city before they boarded the Royal Yacht HMS *Britannia* at Pier 2 in Coddington Cove. In the city the Queen paid a visit to historic Trinity Church and dedicated the newly created park to its west as "Queen Anne Square," honoring her predecessor of the early 18th century who had been a patron of the church. Aboard *Britannia* Queen Elizabeth hosted an official dinner for President and Mrs. Gerald Ford. At midnight, yacht *Britannia*, brilliantly lighted and escorted by British and U.S. warships, sailed under Newport bridge for Boston and that city's Bicentennial festivities.

In August 1978 reenactment of the Battle of Rhode Island brought a large number of re-created historic New England military units together, including the renowned 1st Rhode Island Regiment, to parade in Portsmouth and refight the battle. The action included a mock naval battle north of Melville between Newport's *Rose* and the recently constructed Continental sloop *Providence*. The *Rose*, a replica of the 18th-century British frigate which patrolled the waters of Narragansett Bay in the years leading up to the American Revolution, was built in Lunenberg, Nova Scotia, by Newport resident John Millar. The *Providence*, built by Seaport '76 Foundation, was a modern, operational reproduction of sloop *Katy*, first ship of Rhode Island's pre-Revolutionary Navy, Rhode Island's first contribution to the infant Continental Navy and the first combat command of Captain John Paul Jones. Based in Newport, *Providence* operates each summer on historical and sail training missions in ports from Florida to the Great Lakes.

July 13, 1980, marked the two hundredth anniversary of the arrival in Newport of General Rochambeau with his French regiments. The French missile cruiser *Suffren* and frigate *Aconit* berthed at Coddington Cove. Celebrations included reenactment of the landing in 1780 at King Park, where a statue of Gen. Rochambeau stands, and a special commemorative postcard issued by the U.S. Postal Service. Further 200-year memories of the French took place the following May with the reenactment of Rochambeau's march from Newport to Yorktown, Virginia.

*"Chado," or the Way of Tea. A demonstration held as part of the Black Ships Festival 1991.* Courtesy of the Japan-America Society and Black Ships Festival of Rhode Island, Inc.

Commodore Matthew Calbraith Perry, younger brother of Oliver Hazard Perry, is memorialized as a Newport citizen in Touro Park. The younger Perry, when in command of the Navy's East India Squadron, opened Japan to the western world in 1854. The centennial of this event in 1955 was followed by special observances in both Japan and the United States. In recent years Newport has remembered Perry with a Black Ships Festival, covering a two-week period of Japanese-American cultural and historic events. Each year since 1955 U.S. Navy units have visited Shimoda, where Perry successfully negotiated the treaty of Kanagawa. In 1984 Mayor Patrick Kirby led a Newport delegation to Shimoda, now a sister city of Newport, and Japanese diplomats come annually to Newport for the Black Ships Festival, culminating in a formal ceremony at the Perry statue. In 1985 warships of the Japanese Defense Forces with officer trainees embarked visited Newport during this celebration.

The religious freedom which Roger Williams brought with him to Rhode Island in 1636 was noted in 1982 when the United States issued a special commemorative stamp honoring Touro Synagogue, oldest in continental North America. The First Day Cover sales set a national record with collectors flocking into the city. Neighboring Trinity Church on Spring Street became 250 years old in 1978 and in 1986 underwent a $2.5 million major rehabilitation and strengthening of its historic structure. Trinity, the oldest of Newport's churches in continuous use, was the site of a special patriotic Rhode Island Independence Day service in 1975 and for the next ten years. That ceremony is continued annually at the Congregational Church two blocks away on Spring Street.

## SAILING IN THE BAY AND BEYOND

In the 1970s Newporters assumed they would be regularly hosting America's Cup Races as triennial events because the Cup would naturally remain safely in the possession of the New York Yacht Club.

*The last America's Cup Race in Newport, when* Australia II *(right) beat* Liberty *(left) in the finals in 1983. This was the first time the Cup had been captured by a challenger since the United States challenged the British in 1851 and won.*
Photograph copyright John. T. Hopf.

Races in the summers of 1977 and 1980 found the Australians besting French, Swedish and British challengers, and then being defeated by the New York Yacht Club's defending entry *Courageous* in 1977 and *Freedom* in 1980.

1983, however, brought the unthinkable. Australia again beat challengers from Britain, France, Italy and Canada in the preliminary races. But the 25th America's Cup Races, held in mid-September, ended on September 26th when *Australia II*, with its famous and secret "winged keel," beat the American defender *Liberty* in the seventh race, and the "Auld Mug" went down under to the Royal Perth Yacht Club. By 1987, when the San Diego Yacht Club retrieved the Cup off Perth, Australia, Newport's chances of hosting another series of races had all but disappeared.

Despite many fears, the loss of America's Cup competition has had little overall effect on Newport's yachting life. Narragansett Bay seems to be busier than ever with large and small sailing craft. The biennial Newport-Bermuda race each June brought increasing numbers of contestants in the six classes. Olympic sailing trials in 1988 brought a large number of entries. Single-handed races, trans-Atlantic and round-the-world races are using Newport as starting and finishing port, setting up communications and data centers through the small Goat Island Yacht Club. The American Sail Training Association (ASTA), dedicated to training our youth in ocean sailing, and Sail Newport, organized in 1983 to promote and administer sailing competition in the Bay as well as sailing instruction and small boat availability for tourist rental, have both contributed to the continued strength of interest in yachting. The Museum of Yachting, located in a former artillery mule barn at Fort Adams, opened in 1984 with photographs and exhibits of yachts and models famous in American yachting history. In 1986 *Shamrock V*, Sir Thomas Lipton's America's Cup challenger in 1930, was presented to the Museum and now berths year round in Newport. During the summers of 1989 and 1990 the restored "J" boats *Endeavour* and *Shamrock V* met in the first of a series of races that have revived a bygone era in yacht racing. This rivalry was continued in the summer of 1990 with a series of races along the East Coast.

The ecology of Narragansett Bay and its preservation for commercial and recreational sailors has received increasing attention. Led by Save the Bay, a twenty-year-old non-profit group which continues to campaign vigorously for a cleaner bay, Rhode Island's leaders have generally fallen in step towards environmental goals. Continued use of the Bay and Newport's waterfront by commercial fishermen, while still emphasized by both political parties, has, however, lost ground. Newport's waterfront shipyards began to close as their wharves were taken over for condominium, hotel and marina development. Remaining shipyards are up the bay, far less convenient for fishermen and yacht owners alike.

*George and Manuel Mendonsa of Tallman and Mack Trap Fishing Company mending their nets, 1991.* Photograph copyright Jennifer Murray.

## HISTORY, CULTURE AND EDUCATION

The public school system boasts a highly professional, well-paid faculty and numerous programs for special interests or needs. Yet the physical facilities of several school buildings are obsolete and pressures on the taxpayer and tourist dollars continue to grow. As in other U.S. cities of similar size, Newport's schools become more and more expensive in spite of consolidation and cost-cutting measures.

The once strong parochial school system has contracted in recent years, and St. Joseph's, Jesus Savior, De La Salle Academy and St. Catherine's are all Catholic schools that have been forced to close. Three important parochial schools remain on the Island; the Portsmouth Abbey, founded by John Diman as a priory, St. Philomena's, also in Portsmouth, and the Cluny School off Harrison Avenue in Newport. There are also a number of outstanding private schools in the area. St. George's School, a fully accredited college preparatory school, moved to Middletown from Newport in the autumn of 1901. St. Michael's and The New School provide for younger students.

*The J.N.A. Griswold House, designed by Richard Morris Hunt in 1862, now the home of the Newport Art Museum.* NHS P585.

Salve Regina, the city's only college, continued its growth toward excellence and became a fully accredited university in 1991. The same year saw the completion of a new library complex for the school on the grounds of the well-known estate "Wakehurst."

In addition, other Newport organizations continued recording state and local history, conserving records and interpreting Newport's history to an ever wider audience. The Newport Historical Society took the lead in this, with exhibits, in-house programs on all aspects of the city's past, educational outreach programs, oral history projects and Walking Tours of Historic Newport. Plans were drawn up for moving the Historical Society's internationally important collection of artifacts and manuscripts to a new facility adjacent to the Friends Meeting House.

In 1987 the Redwood Library on Bellevue Avenue opened an additional wing with storage space for another 25,000 volumes. Newport's Public Library added to its collection and is outgrowing the building it first occupied in 1968. The 76-year-old Newport Art Association re-organized itself as the Newport Art Museum in 1983. Its growing collection, with a special focus on Newport's artists, has been served by the construction of a major new gallery wing which was completed in 1991.

The Rhode Island Shakespeare Theater (TRIST) and The Incredibly Far Off Broadway Ensemble Theater are the lone dramatic survivors of the flourishing theater scene of the 1980s. Resident in Newport for ten of its twenty years, The Rhode Island Shakespeare Theater continues to bring live classical drama to New England audiences, while Newport's own dance troupe, Island Moving Company, has attracted a statewide following.

Today Fort Adams, headquarters and largest unit in the defenses of Narragansett Bay for more than a century, is composed of two sections: a Rhode Island State Park and an area of naval housing used by staff officers and students at the Naval War College. The large Wherry Housing Project, built on the Fort's main parade ground in 1953, was torn down in the mid-1970s after providing housing for hundreds of Navy families for twenty years. Some 100 families now occupy the old Army quarters along the parade ground and new apartments built along the bay's entrance. The original commanding officer's quarters is known as Eisenhower House after its use by the President during the summers of 1957 and 1960. The building has become the administration building for the State Park, which includes new fishing and boating piers, a beach and areas for concerts and other events.

Weather in recent years has been generally kind to Newport with a few exceptional storms. In late September 1985 Hurricane Gloria swept up the Atlantic Coast, fortunately striking Narragansett Bay at a period of low tide. There was minimum flooding effect and most of the damage occurred in small boats at their moorings. In February 1978 a strong blizzard smothered New England for several days. Business on Aquidneck Island came to a standstill for a period, and the state's major highways were opened with the help of regular Army and National Guard engineer troops. In August 1991 Hurricane Bob rushed up the east coast of the United States and slammed into Newport County with a vengeance. Damage throughout the state exceeded 20 million dollars, with loss to public lands in Newport alone over 6 million dollars, making it the third worst storm of the century after the Hurricane of 1938 and Hurricane Carol in 1954. Throughout the period, adequate water supply has remained a problem. Local ponds become low too soon in the general pattern of dry summers, making Newport more and more dependent on a single pipeline under the Sakonnet River.

1971 saw the advent of an annual event in Newport to celebrate the Christmas season. "Christmas in Newport," run by a committee composed of volunteers and supported by the Newport Chamber of Commerce, provides a full month of events in December to bring visitors to Newport and gives aid for the city's charitable organizations. All segments of the city are represented in the events which

*Long Wharf following the hurricane of September 1938.* NHS P670.

begin with the lighting of the city's Christmas tree on Washington
Square each December 1. Many households join in the celebration
by putting a single white candle in each window through the end of
the Christmas season on January 6, the Feast of the Epiphany. Lighting of the city is confined to pure white lights in the historic areas,
and on occasion guides in the old homes open for inspection are in
colonial dress. The mansions of the Preservation Society are decorat-
ed especially for public viewing. There are concerts in various churches
and an ecumenical pre-Christmas service of carols in historic Trinity
Church, with choirs from seven or eight congregations taking part.
The cooperative spirit so evident in this month-long event will be
essential to all of the challenges Newport faces as it looks toward its
future.

　　Not every new development was as bright as Christmas in
Newport, however. On June 23, 1989, Newport's 350th anniversary
year, the Greek oil tanker *World Prodigy* ran aground on Brenton Reef
and over a quarter of a million gallons of home heating oil flowed into
the Atlantic Ocean and Narragansett Bay. Tides, winds and quick action
by the U.S. Coast Guard contained much of the spill. Amazingly, few
beaches suffered real damage. This accident did bring home to all the
threat that hangs over our coasts as oil remains a primary source of
energy throughout the world. It also illustrates how Newport's rela-
tionship with the sea — so important throughout the city's history
— has been one fraught with danger as well as beauty and joy.

## POSTSCRIPT

In 1976 Cham Jefferys wrote in conclusion to his historical sketch that this "little old lady by the sea" has survived through thick and thin, boom and bust, war and peace, fair weather and foul with violent storms. In the past Newport has usually found a way of capitalizing on change and there seems to be an excellent chance that she will continue to weather the various storms that affect her to good advantage.

As Newport looks to the next century, the road ahead for the city will not be easy, but if the past is any indication, Newport will continue to thrive, working through the ups and downs, preserving the nationally significant historic architecture from 1675 to the present which makes it unique, trying to balance the needs of a city committed to tourism with those of a city equally committed to making it a wonderful place to live year round.

*The Brick Market, designed by Peter Harrison in 1762, now the Museum of Newport History operated by the Newport Historical Society. This photograph is part of a set commissioned by the 19th-century architect Charles McKim of the firm McKim, Mead and White in the 1870s in which he demonstrated his fascination with colonial Newport.* NHS P168.

# Index

## A